MOVING MOUNTAINS

DISCOVER THE MOUNTAIN IN YOU

JULIE MILES LEWIS

Moving Mountains

First published in 2016 by

Panoma Press Ltd
48 St Vincent Drive, St Albans, Herts, AL1 5SJ, UK
info@panomapress.com
www.panomapress.com

Book design and layout by Neil Coe.

Printed on acid-free paper from managed forests.

ISBN 978-1-784520-89-2

The right of Julie Miles Lewis to be identified as the author of this work has been asserted in accordance with sections 77 and 78 of the Copyright, Designs and Patents Act 1988.

A CIP catalogue record for this book is available from the British Library.

This book is available online and in bookstores.

DEDICATION

For my parents, Reginald and Dorothy Vickers

Thank you for the gift of life; for believing in me before I even believed in myself. Although I have been the one to live and wander furthest away from home, know that you have a special place in my heart; you are with me on the highest mountains, in the deepest oceans, the widest deserts, in fact, wherever I go!

I love you more than words can ever express.

For my sisters Jane, Susan and my brother Paul.

For Calin, your love is the answer.

For Alice, your strength and spirit live on within me.

For my favourite Doctor, Dr. Ron.G Lewis.

To all the amazing people I have had the pleasure of working and sharing so many adventures with

YOU the reader!

Namaste

FOREWARNED!

Warning – you might want to climb a mountain after reading this book, let me know when you do!

I know there is a mountain within you even when you think there isn't one, there is. I speak from personal experience of digging deep to find it. The question is can you see and draw on the strength from it within yourself? When life is weighing you down and you feel stuck in a valley or standing still at base camp, start thinking about the qualities you associate with a mountain: strong, resilient, sacred, magical, confident, able to withstand the wind, rain, snow, thunder and lightning and still stand tall, welcoming the sun kissing its peak, awakening to a new day full of potential – that's the mountain in YOU. The harsh weather shapes the mountain, washes away all the loose stones, carves out new gullies and paths – much like the challenges we face shaping our lives.

I trust you will realise that you are a Mountain and can move any mountains that stand in your way on the path to pure joy, love, health, success and happiness in all that you do, wherever you do it and with whom you do it!

I know you will find the way the minute you start MOVING

THE ONLY WAY IS UP

Jules

"Stand like mountain, flow like water."

– Lao Tzu

ACKNOWLEDGMENTS

This could take a while, however I will do my best to keep it ZEN.

Thanks go to:

First draft reviewers:

Jo Simpson, Wendy Hulbert, Alison Price, Catherine Musto, Jo Macdonald, Cordelia De Rojas, Dr Oudi Abouchacra, Jennifer Ann Gordon and Karin Malmstrom.

Images

Astrid Van Der Knaap – Front cover image

Karissa Lewes – Author Picture

Neil Coe – illustrations with each chapter

Story contributors in order as they appear in the book:

Jannike Moe, Bradley Erasmus, Debbie Nicol, Isobel McArthur, Catherine Musto, Sandi Saksena, Tricia Evans, Liz Keaney, Santiago Garcia, Nicci Roscoe, Alison Price, Ann Holliday, Dr Ginny Whitelaw, Dr Rosalind Buckton-Tucker, Louise Halmakan, Mike Hoff, Wendy Hulbert, Karin Malmstrom, Val Wiggett, Nicholla Henderson-Hall, Michael Catchpole, Gamze Hakli Geray, Mark Evans MBE, Billie Mobyaed, Jo Simpson, Dr Oudi Abouchacra, Carol Talbot, Reem Ghannoum, Wouter Kingma.

I would also like to thank the people whose stories we could not fit in this time round; to have included them would have meant doubling the size of the book! With your kind permission your stories will be posted on our Moving Mountains blog complete with pictures to complement your story.

CONTENTS

INTRODUCTION

I have been talking about writing a book for a long time! I think a lot of people do yet never get started, or never finish what they started. I was one of them until now! I am totally gobsmacked that this book is finally in print and published. What seemed like a good idea at the time soon became a huge mountain to climb, and the only way was up, one word at a time. For someone who loves speaking and using lots of pictures in presentations, you can begin to understand why writing a book with no pictures was an interesting challenge for me

This book is a way of sharing my passion for people, personal development and the great outdoors. I trust the combination of my own story, stories of friends and clients and the fun, yet thought-provoking development exercises will enable you to move any mountains you face, access the mountain in you and maybe even inspire you to climb one.

How to get the most out of this book

1. I highly recommend you get yourself a journal to make additional notes as you read through each chapter and complete the exercises. This book and a journal make great working partners, keep them close together.

2. Have a highlighter pen handy when you are reading, highlight any words, sentences, stories or quotes that really speak to you so it's easy to dip back into them again.

3. Get yourself a small box to use when you get to Chapter 3, this can be as simple or ornate as you like. I also suggest you buy a clear quartz crystal or have something that symbolises clarity to hold in your left hand for one of the exercises in Chapter 3. Have different coloured post-it notes at hand.

4. Get yourself a globe and a map of the world – you'll see why when you get to Chapter 5!

5. At the end of each chapter I have suggested that you take time out to meditate before moving on to the next chapter. Start with five minutes and build up each day to 20-30 minutes or more. Simply close your eyes, sit still, breathe normally and let any thoughts pass through you as you settle into a deep calm state. Give yourself the gift of silence and stillness everyday.

6. At the end of each chapter you will see the words 'Come to your senses'. This is an invitation to heighten your self-awareness through the senses of sight, sound, smell, taste and touch linked to the chapter you have read. After your meditation tap into your senses and note any insights in your journal.

7. Each chapter comes with a suggested affirmation for you to use. Have fun creating some of your own to reinforce the essence of the chapter. Affirmations are positive statements said in the present tense suggesting that something is already so. They are best combined with deep breathing to get the effect of a relaxed body and focused mind.

8. The Power of Three exercise at the end of each chapter will help you clarify what you intend to stop, start and continue doing with reference to the chapter.

9. Finally, you will find a prompt to write your own story relating to the chapter you have just read. You are also encouraged to think about what you are excited, committed and grateful about in relation to each chapter.

Lots to read, think and write about, so turn the page and let's get moving.

START WITH WHAT YOU'VE GOT

CHAPTER 1

ONE STEP AT A TIME

"The journey of a thousand miles
begins with a single step."

– Lao Tzu

WELL DONE! You have just taken the first step to accessing the mountain in you and 'moving on' by picking up this book. What moved you to do so? The title, the cover, the overview on the back? Maybe you've been waiting for a reinforcement sign from the universe that it's time to get moving and make some changes in your personal or professional life – this book is your sign! Whatever it was that moved you to pick up this book, THANK YOU.

MOVING SINCE 1962

It started when I came into the world on 7 April 1962 as a newborn – I have been moving ever since! From being a newborn to a toddler, crawler, walker, from childhood into teens, to adolescence, young woman, university student, degree graduate, fitness consultant, semi-professional body builder, college lecturer, sports and beach

resort manager, golf club sales and **PR** manager, self-employed fitness consultant, business development manager, mountain climber, expedition leader, peak performance coach, professional speaker – and now an aspiring author!

I experienced getting out of my comfort zone when I left home at the age of 11 to go to a Quaker school in West Yorkshire as a boarder where I stayed until I was 18. I went on to study Sports Science at the University of Sheffield, graduated, moved into my first job and took my first overseas posting in Kuwait at the age of 27. I moved pretty quickly when Iraq invaded Kuwait in August 1990 (after three weeks of hiding, a group of us fled across the desert into Saudi then on to our home countries). I guess that was my earliest adventure. After four years in the UK I moved back to Kuwait in 1994, to Dubai in 1997, Hong Kong in 2010 and have now lived in Abu Dhabi for the last three years. During all of this I got married in 1990, was unexpectedly widowed in 1998 and, after sorting out my heart and head again, I re-married, to Calin in 2008. Calin and I moved homes eight times in three years (not recommended!).

Honestly, I do find it hard to sit still for long periods of time. When I was a child, Dad would challenge me to sit still; he used to say he would give me £5 if I sat still for more than 10 minutes. When I needed some extra pocket money I did actually manage to sit still (for at least 10 minutes!).

During a Zen Leadership training course I managed to sit in zazen (sitting meditation) for 50 minutes! Now I happily sit for 20 minutes zazen every day, sometimes twice a day – amazing!

Through Mountain High I have been on the move leading over 55 expeditions to more than 20 countries to include seven expeditions to the Arctic and two to Antarctica. I have joined several active movements as a women's health advocate, moved many metaphorical mountains and climbed 19 real ones. I am

often moved to sing, laugh, dance, cry (tears of joy and sadness) and have been known to try out colonics – where funnily enough even the therapist said, "Enjoy your movement," to which I replied, "Yes – I always do!" Enough said on this topic!

This book was truly written on the move. It's hard to believe that after the first kick-start session I had with Mindy on 3 September 2015 I travelled to five countries within seven weeks and just before the first draft was sent out to review I was on my way to Antarctica – pretty mad really. It's fair to say I am comfortable with moving and able, in one way or another, to enable others to get moving!

LET'S GET MOVING

So, you and I are now going on a fabulous journey together and I am delighted to be your guide on this adventure. Just imagine me being right by your side every time you hold this book in your hand; even when you are not holding it, my thoughts and positive energy are reaching out to you wherever you are in the world as you move in, on, up, out and beyond towards your wildest dreams and, in the process, discover the mountain within you. My deepest wish is that one day we will meet so you can share your 'move on and inner mountain' success stories in person.

THE MOUNTAIN IN ME

In 2001 I had the opportunity to go on an educational trip to Malaysia to explore what the country had to offer with a view to bringing groups over from the Middle East. At the time I had just started working for an adventure travel company as a business development manager. It was during this trip that I first set eyes on Mount Kota Kinabalu in Sabah, Malaysian Borneo. Something about the mountain was definitely calling to my soul; it was almost as if I were seeing a reflection of myself in the mountain. Whatever it was, the mountain had my name all over it and to this day I remember having a strong gut feeling that I was destined to come back and climb it. I asked our guide how long it would take to climb the mountain and the best time to come and climb; as soon as he mentioned April as a good month I decided that this would be a unique way to celebrate my 40th birthday the following year. Just for the record, I think birthdays are always a good time to do something totally different that takes you out of your everyday world. During this same trip we also visited Sarawak and watched the longboat races on the Kuching River. Again my imagination ran wild, more questions were asked and I made the decision that as well as climbing the highest mountain in South East Asia, I would bring a team of women and men to race in the Sarawak Regatta. We spent 10 fabulous days in Malaysia and when we got back to Dubai I started making plans for 2002 – a mountain to climb and a Regatta to race in!

4095 METRES ABOVE SEA LEVEL

Fast forward to April 2002: I find myself at 4095 metres above sea level on the summit of Mount Kota Kinabalu celebrating my 40th birthday with five other women whom I had managed to persuade to join me. Having *Happy Birthday* sung to me at 5.30 in the morning on top of the mountain was a pretty special way to mark the beginning of life at 40! The sun was up, the clouds had cleared and I was feeling on top of the world... and totally fabulous at 40.

All the planning and preparation had paid off: months of training in the gym, reading up about the mountain, making sure we had the right clothing and equipment, choosing a guide – all the things you do to increase your chance of success. One by one we all picked a spot on the summit to capture our moment of glory and achievement. As you might have already guessed, we had all perfected the 'rocky pose': arms outstretched, head up with big smiles on our faces – feeling on top of the world. It was during my rocky pose moment that I had a flash of inspiration.

There I was on top of a mountain, feeling totally alive and connected to nature, on a natural high. I had discovered the mountain in me so the question to myself was: how about setting up a company called Mountain High to inspire and encourage more women to discover the mountain within themselves? The idea for Mountain High was born at 4095m; the quest was to make it a reality.

On the way down from the mountain I sensed that something very significant had shifted within me: a newfound sense of courage and confidence to step out and make a difference, to leave a positive footprint on the planet through my passion for people and the outdoors in a unique way. It's fair to say that through climbing the mountain I had found a new sense of clarity, direction and purpose for my life and was totally open to the possibilities ahead.

Where do you get your flashes of inspiration?

Safely back at base camp we all looked up to the mountain one more time as we collected our Summit Certificates from the National Park office. Time to kick off our hiking boots, peel off our socks, slip into flip-flops, pile on to the minibus and head to the Rasa Ria Hotel and resort for celebration drinks and well deserved massages. That night we sat out on the beach at the resort, again finding ourselves drawn to look up at the mountain we had stood on top of earlier – what a difference a day makes! We tucked into dinner followed by birthday cake and champagne as we recounted our magical journey. Change was in the air!

BACK IN DUBAI

Days later, when we were back in Dubai, I had a call from a journalist who had heard about my mission to climb a mountain for my 40th birthday and wanted to write an article for the *Gulf News*. I had no idea that my life-changing experience would be of interest to so many people. A week later the story was in print and all of a sudden I was getting calls from other women who also wanted to do something special to mark their 40th birthday.

One of the calls came from Jannike, who quickly became my soul sister, a Norwegian woman who shared the same love of the great outdoors that I had. We met for a coffee, talked for hours, played around with several ideas on where to go and which mountain to climb. Eventually we came up with the concept of the *Everest Women's Challenge*: a trek to Everest Base Camp in 2003 to celebrate the 50th anniversary of Everest – 18 women, 18 days, trekking to 18,000ft. Our meeting came at a time in our lives when we were both looking for something more, a new way of living, a new way of being, a new way to inspire more women to realise their own ambitions and live out their wildest dreams.

JANNIKE'S STORY

Meeting Julie became the start of a new life. I had had a colourful youth with lots of fun adventures – but the last seven years I had forgotten who I was. I had had eight failed IVF attempts, living with a husband whose business was going bust and me not being very well at all. In the middle of all this we had adopted a gorgeous girl from Guatemala. The adoption of Maria was the only 'up' during this time period.

I was turning 40 and felt that I had very much put myself on a shelf. I desperately needed to do something that would set a mark in my life. In the summer of 2002 I got in touch with Jules – how little did we know at the time just what we were going to do and achieve in the years to come.

Our lives weaved into each other's at just the right time. Jules was on a high from having climbed her first mountain and was keen to do more and I was hungry to get moving again. Together we gave birth to our first project – The Everest Women's Challenge. What was meant to be an escape for me developed into a massive media campaign involving the whole community. We did the most amazing fund-raising event on a beautiful ship which was docked in Dubai at the time and attracted lots of generous people who were prepared to dig deep into their pockets to support the purchase of a mobile breast-screening unit, which the team had committed to fund raise for.

Straight after the 'talk of the town party' we left for Nepal. What a contrast! We were on our way to experience something we would never forget – our first adventure to such a special place. When we landed at Lukla (regarded as the world's second most dangerous airport) Jules and I looked at each other and we just knew there and then that this was the start of something very special and never-ending.

Jannike Moe

*"Begin what you want to do now.
We are not living in eternity.*

*We only have this moment, sparkling like a star
in our hand and melting like a snowflake."*

– Sir Francis Bacon

THE ONLY WAY IS UP

One year after my first mountain climb I found myself in Nepal with 17 amazing women, all different nationalities and ages, wearing pink bandanas (for breast cancer awareness) and singing *The Only Way is Up* all the way to Everest Base Camp at 5370m. We chose to raise awareness and funds for breast cancer as both Jannike and I had friends that had been affected by it. By helping to purchase a mobile screening unit it would allow more women to take charge of their breast health and have access to mammograms. This trek turned out to be the catalyst for so many of the women on the expedition to make some pretty big moves in their lives: to commit to a relationship, to leave a relationship, to leave a job, start a business, and for one woman a whole new life in New Zealand. For me the 18 days in the mountains was the final nudge to leave my job and start Mountain High; the rest, as they say, is history!

From that first mountain climb on Kinabalu to meeting my soul sister Jannike, together we had impacted the lives of 16 other women to get moving on their own ambitions, step out of their comfort zone and explore their own place in the world.

IT TAKES SMALL STEPS TO ACCOMPLISH THE BIG THINGS IN LIFE

I am often asked, "How do you climb a mountain?" Very simply, the answer is, "One step at a time." The moment you start walking the mountain comes to you. Setting and maintaining a steady pace on the mountain and knowing when to speed up or slow down is crucial to success. This applies to many things in life. I have seen people race up a mountain and then struggle to make it to the summit or actually have to turn back as their bodies have not been able to acclimatise to the altitude. It takes small consistent steps to reach the summit and achieve the big things in life.

SLOW DOWN AND ARRIVE SOONER

I remember the first time I took a group to climb Kilimanjaro back in 2005. The team commented on some of the other groups who were racing ahead of us on the mountain, they were always the first into camp and openly bragged about how easy it was. Two days later most of them were experiencing nausea, headaches and actually had to go back down the mountain to prevent their altitude sickness getting worse. The tortoise and the hare story springs to mind – slow down and arrive sooner. As with many things in life, as long as you keep moving forward you will get there in the end. On a mountain, and in life, it pays to be patient and enjoy the journey rather than race ahead without stopping to smell the roses and take in the scenery along the way.

THE ONLY WAY TO THE TOP IS ONE STEP AT A TIME

Mountain climbing is like so many other skill-based sport activities in that you need to train specifically for what you intend to do. If you want to run a marathon you need to start a training programme that will build you up to being able to run the full distance on the day of the event. If you want to play a decent round of golf you need to start with lessons then practice, practice, practice. If you want to go diving it's wise to sign up for an open water course and get all the basics under your belt.

If you are thinking about changing career then it makes sense to start learning the new skills that will allow you to make the transition. If you want to lose weight you need to set a plan in place to do it over a period of time and make exercise and good nutrition part of your lifestyle versus starving yourself for a few days and expecting long-term results. From my experience, taking this one step at a time fills the journey with peace and success instead of stress and setbacks.

My adventure was writing this book – a stretch goal so a little out of my comfort zone. If you want to write a book, decide on the topic, something you are passionate about, have an outline plan in place before you start writing and find yourself a mentor, coach, friend, or writers' group who will help you along the way. I think you get the idea of what I am trying to suggest here so think about what you would like to do and what your first step will be to reach your goal.

NO SHORTCUTS

On one particularly challenging trek a potential client asked me about joining the expedition. However, she had not done any training, had never been hiking, didn't own a pair of hiking boots but was desperate to come, so much so that she offered to pay double the cost of the actual trip. As well as having an impact on the team who had been training together for four months prior to the trip, taking her on with no prior experience or training would have been setting her up for failure. Diplomatically I had to turn the request down. I suggested a training programme for her and agreed to get together again in three months' time after putting in the work needed to make it possible to join such trips, and actually enjoy the journey. I am pleased to say she did train and go on to climb several mountains. As far as I know there are no shortcuts to excellence and peak performance; it takes consistent daily action, discipline and commitment. Let me know if you think otherwise.

"Nature does not hurry yet everything is accomplished."

– Lao Tzu

OUT OF THE FAT INTO THE FIRE

Moving away from mountains and on to everyday life scenarios, how many people do you know that have jumped out of one relationship into another without really spending time on their own or thinking about what they really want or what caused the relationship to go off track in the first place? How often have you felt the need to fill the void, to jump right into another job, another relationship, another purchase that you think will make you happy rather than taking the time to reflect on your past choices and make new ones based on a clear plan rather than a spur of the moment whim? Take a moment to reflect on any setbacks you have faced because you failed to research and plan and how many successes you have experienced because you did have a step-by-step plan. Note them down in your journal; just by being more aware you can change or course-correct your life's direction without getting burnt.

There is a big difference in the outcome when you plan ahead instead of leaping into something with no prior thought or training. By the same token, I know that at some point along the way a quantum leap is a must – that is, to stop talking and start doing. What have you been thinking, planning and training for?

Whatever it is, it might be useful for you to use the same mantra I did for finally getting started on this book – here it is: LESS TALK – MORE ACTION!

MAKING CAREER CHANGES

It's pretty normal to feel insecure about making a career transition. I know lots of people who feel stuck in a job that offers financial security but not much else. Maybe you have outgrown a profession you once loved or find yourself wrestling with insecurities about making a change, especially when your change might impact people you love or your financial responsibilities. Some people would suggest to just quit, and if you have the financial means to do this maybe this is right for you. If not, how about using your evenings, weekends and holidays to learn, practise and certify in a new skill that will carry you forward into the next chapter of your life?

When I first started Mountain High I took a part-time job on a temporary contract. This helped to make sure I could at least cover my basic living expenses in the start-up phase. Within six months I was able to let this go and focus 100% on Mountain High projects. What can you do to get started?

POSITIVE POSSIBILITIES

When you are thinking about making a change, instead of focusing on what might happen in a negative sense, allow yourself to imagine all the new positive possibilities that come with living your purpose and start taking daily action to move you towards your dream career, and know that however small the steps, it's up to you to take them… so get moving!

TAKE TIME DAILY TO QUIET YOUR MIND – TUNE INTO YOUR INNER MOUNTAIN

Decide on what you want to be, do and have. Be very specific about what it is you want to achieve, when you want to achieve it, why you want to achieve it, who can help you achieve it and what you need to do on a daily, weekly or monthly basis to achieve it. Focus your time, energy and attention on a skill or a training course that is linked to what you want to do. Maybe it's a hobby that you can turn into an occupation. Connect with someone who is already doing what you want to do and ask for their advice, read books on the topic, join groups that are aligned with your goal. Take time out to tune into your inner mountain of resources, tap into your intuition and act on its guidance.

NEW BEGINNINGS

When you are in the midst of letting go to make room for the new, it's not uncommon to find yourself burdened by a barrage of obstacles: the things or people on your path that can slow you down or even keep you away from your goal. Whenever you think about quitting, stop and ask yourself why you started in the first place – you know that compelling reason why you wanted to get moving on to a new chapter of your life. In my experience, feelings of self-doubt and heartache are all part of the new beginning process; as the saying goes, what doesn't kill you will make you stronger. What I do know is that when you have the courage to take the first step and seek the support of others to help you along the way, you can cover new ground very quickly.

When you start taking bold action towards your dreams it is not always possible or necessary to see the entire path ahead. Once you take that first step you often find that new energy enters and the next steps become so much clearer; with every step you take you will find that you generate more momentum. Whenever you are faced with what seems an overwhelming challenge, resist the urge to back away or procrastinate; break it down into a series of smaller achievable steps and celebrate each step.

The most important part of any project or undertaking is the beginning. What new beginnings are calling you? Your job is to CHOOSE and BEGIN.

"When you are inspired by some great purpose, some extraordinary project, all your thoughts break their bonds: Your mind transcends limitations, your consciousness expands in every direction, and you find yourself in a new, great and wonderful world.

Dormant forces, faculties and talents become alive, and you discover yourself to be a greater person by far than you ever dreamed yourself to be."

– Patanjali

START WITH WHAT YOU'VE GOT

The same year we climbed Kota Kinabalu in Malaysia we also took a team from Dubai to race in the Sarawak Regatta. With no longboats available for training in Dubai we had to make the best of what we could find which, believe it or not, was a steel barrel raft welded together by one of my friends. It was nothing like a longboat but it was a start and allowed us to get out on the water and paddle. When we got on to the raft the paint was still wet – our keenness to start using it resulted in white streaks of paint on our tush! It was hard to stay on the barrels so we cut up some yoga mats and stuck them around the barrels to prevent us from slipping off! Eventually we were able to borrow four Canadian canoes to train in; it was only when we got to Sarawak that we were able to sit in a real longboat and practise paddling with a local team. After training on steel barrels and Canadian canoes the longboats were a doddle – so, the moral of this story is *start with what you've got.*

FROM THE SAND TO THE SNOW

In 2007 Jannike and I worked together on a project to take a team of 18 women to the Arctic on a dog sledding expedition. Based on the fact that all the women who came on the trip lived in the UAE (United Arab Emirates) it was important for us to get used to being in the snow prior to the trip. Cue Ski Dubai, an indoor ski slope located in the Mall of the Emirates. I asked the marketing manager for permission to use the slopes for training every Saturday morning before they opened to the public; thankfully she agreed and we were able to train together for six weeks prior to heading out to the Arctic. We were the first team of women to get permission to camp out overnight at Ski Dubai! The only thing that was not possible was to have a team of huskies on the slopes (yellow snow not allowed!). Since 2007 we have been able to use the slopes to train teams who have signed up for mountain treks or the Arctic and Antarctica expeditions. One step at a time it was possible to prepare everyone for the transition from the sand to the snow and the heat to the cold. Awesome!

CROSSING THE SANDS OF TIME

In 2014 I teamed up with Mark Evans from Outward Bound Oman and put together the first and only team of women from the UAE and Asia to complete a north to south crossing of the Wahiba sands in Oman. The crossing took us just over four days; we walked a total of just over 115km – one step a time. We were a team of eight women supported by three camels, a Bedouin guide and a Toyota pickup truck. We carried our own supplies, pitched our own tents and made our own meals every day. We had strategy in place and it worked: early wake-up call, hot cup of tea, breakfast, break camp and start walking by 6am. One of the team members kept an eye on time to make sure we were taking a break every 60-90minutes, another team member had the GPS to track out our route and two of the team members set the pace. By delegating tasks we completed the challenge together as a team – albeit complete with blisters! Having a system in place and taking one step at a time made all the difference.

GETTING OUT OF DEBT ONE STEP AT A TIME

While living in Hong Kong we met lots of new people through joining various business networking groups – one of them being Brad who I met through BNI (Business Network International). Brad had an amazing story to share about how he got himself out of debt and had become a US$ millionaire. Sharing his story here highlights that often the challenges we face are not physical such as climbing a mountain or crossing the desert, they are financial and emotional. Managing money can be a challenge for some people; it's easy to live a 'plastic fantastic' life with credit cards and loans. If you are currently facing a financial challenge of your own, this next story will help you get moving out of any financial debt you find yourself in. If it makes you think of someone you know who is struggling, please tell them Brad's story to help them get moving.

I once got myself so far into depressing, debilitating debt that it took me eight years to get back to being solvent again! It then took me only a few years to become a US$ millionaire!

Here's what I learnt: We need to take responsibility for every thought, feeling, action and result that has landed us in the situation in which we find ourselves! It is always far easier to cast the blame outside of ourselves but this gets us nowhere fast.

Remember too that everyone makes mistakes. Making mistakes and learning from them is how you evolve and move forward. Of the top ten entrepreneurs who have become billionaires over the last hundred years, only one (Bill Gates) did not go bankrupt at least once in their lifetime, which shows that even the most successful people in the world have failed, failed big, and used what they learnt to make a comeback. So never beat yourself up. You are actually in good company!

Another important point: always seek out at least one bright aspect of your situation. This gratitude will put you in an abundant state of mind and will help you to attract the resources and support you need to move forward.

Freeing Yourself from Debt – The First Steps

- *Acknowledge your mistakes without shaming or blaming yourself. Look for the lesson and the gift.*

- *Take responsibility and change your mindset and behaviour.*

- *Admit your situation to people you trust, asking for their help in getting you to stick to a revised spending plan.*

- *Ask empowering questions, looking for solutions rather than focusing solely on the problems.*

- *Relationships are more important than money. If you borrow money from family or friends, put the details into a simple document, signed and witnessed by a mediator.*

- *PMA – adopt a Positive Mental Attitude – being grateful for the lesson and all that is good in your life, while keeping faith in yourself and your ability to turn things around.*

I wish you all the best! You can do it! You will do it!

Bradley Erasmus – author of *My Journey from $65,000 in debt to my first million*

By the way, Brad took me up on the challenge to bungee jump off the Macau Tower to mark International Women's Day in 2011. It takes a lot of balls to do this – but I guess if you can get over being US$65,000 in debt, bungee jumping off the Macau Tower is a walk in the park! I hasten to add that I did not have the balls to bungee jump. I went for the softer option of a straightforward jump off the edge feet first (I have no intention of doing anything head first unless it's diving into a swimming pool – complete with water in it of course!).

BRIGHT IDEA:

Look at an area of your life that you would like to change – use the power questions below to help you get started.

Know that even the tiniest step in the right direction will get the change process started, and the next steps will get easier and bigger as you go along!

POWER QUESTIONS

1. What do I want to be, do, have?

2. What is my primary focus?

3. What's the first step I need to take?

4. Who can help me, what resources do I need?

5. Why is this important to me?

6. What will happen if I do this?

7. What will happen if I don't do this?

Before you move on to the next chapter write down and take three actions that will move you towards one of your primary goals. Take one step at a time and give each step your complete attention and energy. It's common to feel there are too many things to do, so instead of having a laser beam focus, there is a tendency to do a bit here and a bit there instead of taking on one task or step at a time and getting on with just that step. Kick the habit of chasing three rabbits; chase one, catch it and then start chasing the next one!

Time to switch off and close the book after reading the next lot of instructions. Find a place where you will not be disturbed or distracted, relax, take three deep breaths, sit on a chair or on the floor, close your eyes and meditate for a minimum of five minutes.

I know you can do more – the goal here is to get started and build up to 30 minutes… or more!

When you have finished meditating, open your eyes and in your own time pick up your journal and a pen and start noting down any thoughts or insights linked to this chapter. Self-awareness precedes change and helps you get moving, tap into all your senses, *come to your senses* when you are writing down your thoughts (see, hear, taste, smell, touch and sixth sense – intuition). Once you have done this, open the book again to this page and move on from where you left off. You will be repeating this process at the end of every chapter – so by the end of the book it will be second nature to you!

1. MEDITATE

2. COME TO YOUR SENSES

3. AFFIRMATION
Every Step I take Moves me Closer to my Goal

Remember to create your own and write them in your journal, on post-it notes posted where you can see them, or on the Notes pages at the end of the book. Do this for each of the chapters.

4. POWER OF THREE

What are you going to start, stop and continue doing as a result of reading this chapter?

What's your 'ONE STEP AT A TIME' STORY? Write it now.

What are you excited, committed and grateful about in relation to this chapter? Jot your thoughts down in your journal or on the Notes pages at the end of the book.

ANSWERS FROM
WITHIN

CHAPTER 2

IT'S ALL IN YOU

*"Your work is to discover your greatness and
with all your heart give yourself to it."*

– Buddha

NAMASTE

In Nepal, 'Namaste' is a customary greeting when people meet
or depart from each other. 'Namaste' is spoken with a slight bow
and hands pressed together, palms touching and fingers pointing
upwards, thumbs close to the chest. The meaning behind this
greeting is 'I bow to the divine in you'. In Tibetan the greeting is
'Tashi Delek', which means 'I honour the light in you'.

How do you honour the divine light within you? Do you believe in
yourself and allow the diamond-like brilliance of your individuality
to shine from the depths of your being? Or do you allow your inner
critic (the voice in your head) to override your inner mountain of
resources?

THE MOUNTAIN IN YOU

I know there is a mountain within you – even when you think there isn't one, there is; believe me, I speak from personal experience of digging deep to find it. The question is can you see and draw on the strength from it within yourself? When life is weighing you down and you feel stuck in a metaphorical valley or standing still at base camp, start thinking about the qualities you associate with a mountain: strong, resilient, sacred, magical, confident, able to withstand the wind, rain, snow, thunder and lightning and still stand tall, welcoming the sun kissing its peak, awakening to a new day full of potential – that's the mountain in YOU. The harsh weather shapes the mountain, washes away all the loose stones, carves out new gullies and paths – much like the challenges we face shaping our lives.

"You have a treasure within you that is infinitely greater than anything the world can offer."

– Eckhart Tolle

One of the first steps to achieving everything you want in life is to identify and develop your strengths within your character (your jewels) and set in place an action plan to move forward. This means tapping into all the things you believe are your strengths, for example: resilient, kind, dependable, loving, courageous, patient, good learner, good listener, able to see things through. These are all jewels, some of them might be raw, others may be polished… just know that you have them!

"Knowing others is intelligence;
Knowing yourself is true wisdom.
Mastering others is strength;
mastering yourself is true power."

– Lao Tzu, Tao Te Ching

BRIGHT IDEA:

Stop reading now and grab a pen and several pieces of coloured paper (post-it notes will be fine). Write all your inner resources (strengths/jewels) on each piece of paper then drop them into your treasure chest (buy yourself a small treasure chest or ornate box). If you prefer to stick them on your bathroom mirror so you see them every morning, go for it! If there are resources you feel you need to be able to move on that you currently do not have, list them on different coloured pieces of paper and start thinking about how you can develop them. Look in your treasure box often – especially when you find yourself riddled with any doubts about your inner jewels and gems. It's your time to let them sparkle and shine – NOW!

"The universe buries strange jewels deep within us all,
and then stands back to see if we can find them."

– Elizabeth Gilbert, Big Magic

BE YOURSELF AND BOOST YOUR SELF-ESTEEM

When you feel good about yourself you radiate positive energy, your moods are more balanced, you are able to accept constructive criticism and make healthy life choices; you are also more able to deal with stressful situations. People with high self-esteem believe in themselves, are able to laugh at themselves, are comfortable with change and are willing to take risks and go the extra mile to achieve their goals. The fastest way to boost your self-esteem is to take really good care of yourself, and be yourself – besides, as Oscar Wilde said, "Everyone else is taken."

You can achieve what you truly want, whether that is to make more money, get a better job, enjoy good relationships, write a book, get in shape or grow a business. Sometimes others believe in us before we believe in ourselves; you know, the ones who remind you of all your magical qualities when you can't see them yourself. Who are your raving fans, your cheerleaders, the ones who see all your natural talents and encourage you to draw on them as you pursue your dreams? Just take a moment now and before moving on write a list of their names in your journal and make sure your name is top of the list. Yes – it starts with you being your own raving fan! Make sure you spend time with your cheerleaders – especially when you are having moments of doubt: you know, the times you can only hear your inner critic instead of tapping into your inner mountain.

> *"Always be a first-class version of you instead of a second-rate version of somebody else."*
>
> – Judy Garland

IF YOU CAN DREAM IT YOU CAN DO IT

The fact that you picked up this book shows that you are open to exploring new possibilities. It may sound like a cliché yet within your spirit lies all the strength you will ever need to succeed. I invite you to have the courage to follow your heart and never allow anyone or anything to tame your spirit. Goals are dreams with dates on them; if you can dream it you can do it. Carve out some time daily to daydream – the only limit is your imagination.

Wake up to your greatness.

"When sleeping women wake, mountains move."
– Chinese proverb

TO THE ENDS OF THE EARTH

I met Adila in October 2006 at the Jumeriah Beach Hotel Health Club in Dubai. Dr Houriya Kazim, a breast cancer surgeon, had passed on Adila's contact number and suggested we meet as I was looking for a team of women to go to the Arctic in 2007 as part of the Tickled Pink Series. The goal was to get a multinational team of women together and have at least one breast cancer survivor on the team to reinforce that there is life after cancer and that whatever you set your heart, soul and mind to you can achieve. Having lived in the UAE since 1997 it was important to me that we had at least one Emirati woman with us on the team. As soon as I met Adila I knew she would be with us; she had just come out of a training session and was wearing her martial arts gear, she was a warrior! As we talked through the trip and described what we would be doing – ice caving, snow mobile safari and dog sledding for four days in 360 degrees of pristine wilderness – I could see the sparkle in her eyes. She was going through treatment for breast cancer at the time and had been advised to have a double mastectomy and was due to go to London for the operation within a month. The trip to the Arctic was in April 2007 so there was a good few months between the operation and the expedition. I believed in her the minute we started talking and knew she could do it. We agreed that her sister Samina would come along with her as she was a doctor and a great source of support for Adila.

By joining the expedition, they would be the first two Emirati sisters in the Arctic so modern day history was also in the making – double whammy! Over the next five months we stayed in touch while she was in London recovering from the operation. Daily text messages of love and support, emailing pictures of huskies, of team training at Ski Dubai – all reinforcing my belief and the team's belief in Adila, which in turn supercharged Adila's self-belief. In April 2007 Adila and Samina held the Emirati flag at 78 degrees north in the Norwegian Arctic circle after a three-day dog sledding expedition to the ship in the ice. To this day I remember very clearly seeing Adila standing strong and resilient like a mountain as she managed her sled powered by six huskies, cruising through the snow-covered valleys. I had tears of joy in my eyes as I knew how much it meant for her to be there with Samina. Two months later Adila was also part of the Tickled Pink Paddlers team that won silver medals in the Penang Dragon Boat Festival and has since been to the Arctic three times and joined the Antarctica expedition with us in 2012 – there is no stopping this woman!

"Our deepest fear is not that we are inadequate; our deepest fear is that we are powerful beyond measure."

– Marianne Williamson

ANSWERS FROM WITHIN

This next sentence might sound 'new agey' (by the way, we need a new age), however, I encourage you to trust that you have all the answers within you. Whatever the question is, your intuition has something to tell you! Ask the universe and learn how to listen deeply for the answer.

"Go inside and listen to your body, because your body will never lie to you.

Your mind will play tricks, but the way you feel in your heart, in your guts, is the truth."

– Miguel Ruiz

My friend Debbie went to sleep on a question and woke up with an answer.

My business's legal status was ready for an upgrade. Not only would it have a different classification, but also a trading name! Preparations were well underway for months before, with me choosing the name, designing the logo and investing quite heavily in SEO services. The day was finally here and so were the inspectors!

The inspector reported back: 'This name looks fine for us, yet as it's quite similar to another business partner's trading name, we request you just check with them and present a letter of no objection. Should be no problem.'

Upon receiving the response that was an absolute and resolute 'no', I was a broken woman. I had put so much time, money and effort into this day, and now with the 24-hour deadline looming, options were fading as I crawled into bed and curled up in a ball. One last sentence flowed from my mouth: Please universe! If there's ever any time I need help, it's now!

As the sun rose the next morning, my smile grew bigger and broader. The universe had delivered a solution that I could never ever have thought of! With one slight change in the name, I was to also enjoy three unexpected benefits! It's all in you; learn to trust, let go and watch as the universe creates solutions you could not have even dreamt of!

Debbie Nicol – Director, Business EnMotion

"All the time our warmth and brilliance are right here. We are one blink away from being fully awake."

– Pema Chodrun

 ## BRIGHT IDEA:

Stop reading now, grab a pen and your journal and list the times you have ignored your intuition and note how things turned out. Then write down the times you followed your intuition and how things turned out well. Look over your answers, listen and learn from them and allow yourself to tune into your intuition more often – I have a strong feeling this will work for you!

SELF-RELIANCE

I met so many wonderful people in Dubai, Isobel was one of them. I had been introduced to her through friends and went on to do Reiki training and wellness retreats with her in 2004. I knew things at home were not 100%, however I never really knew how much Isobel was going through at the time. It's amazing how she held her ground, connected to all her inner resources (the mountain within) and got moving.

> *"What lies behind us and what lies before us are tiny matters compared to what lies within us."*
>
> – Ralph Waldo Emerson

Isobel's story

It is a true saying that you never know how strong or resilient you are until pushed to your absolute limits. When the option of staying in a situation becomes more uncomfortable or painful than leaving is the point that you take the leap of faith and dive into your pool of inner strength and courage and leave whatever is destroying your soul.

My own personal experience of finding the determination, strength and energy to leave an extremely abusive, self-confidence destroying relationship, my home of 28 years, friends, and a very successful business to start from scratch in another country tested my resolve beyond measure. Starting a new business, building a new home, making new friends while going through an incredibly difficult divorce gave me the choice of sink or swim. Instead I took this situation and all of the learning from this painful time in my life to become more tenacious to rise up and succeed.

I have taken this life experience and turned it around as an opportunity to grow and develop in all aspects of my life. I have truly moved on. In doing so I am thriving, my business is thriving and I am helping other women find their voice, empowerment and strength to change whatever is not working in their life. What's more I am happily remarried and enjoying the journey. Yes, the journey towards change is not easy, and yes there are obstacles to overcome, however as you tap into all the wonderful gifts that lie within you, is the point of true inner peace, clarity, direction and lack of dependence on anyone but yourself.

Isobel McArthur, Life Transformational Specialist

ACCESSING YOUR INNER MOUNTAIN

There's something about climbing a mountain that mirrors our life journey. There are times when you need to stand strong like a mountain and weather the storm and others when you need to let go and go with the flow. I met Catherine in Dubai when she interviewed me for a teaching post. I didn't get the job however we became great friends and climbed Kilimanjaro together in 2005. The next story shares her experience on Mount Kinabalu. It's a story of inner strength that I totally relate to having climbed the same mountain in 2002.

> *"Everything in the universe is within you.*
> *Ask all from yourself."*
>
> – Rumi

Watching the dawn rise on a new chapter in my life…

Perched on the summit of Mount Kinabalu, I watched the dawn break on a beautiful new day. But this wasn't just any ordinary day; I was effectively watching the dawn rise on a new chapter in my life. Later that day my divorce hearing was coming up before a UK court. Spending a few minutes in mindful reflection gave me the space to see that, much like the gruelling ascent of the mountain I'd just climbed, the difficulties of the past few years were behind me too. I was now, physically and mentally, at a new height – a place of clarity and vision, where possibilities were boundless. I knew I'd found the strength and courage to reach not only the summit of a real mountain but, even more importantly, I had also reached the summit of my inner mountain.

My upward climb of either mountain was by no means easy. I had to dig deep to find the strength, especially in the dark days after discovering my husband's affair. The burning hurt of betrayal, and the pain and sadness of seeing my hopes and dreams crushed, left me feeling deeply wounded. When, like on the real mountain, the terrain immediately in front of me seemed insurmountable I effectively had two choices: give up or carry on. On the final ascent of Mt. Kinabalu it was cold and dark and tough; companions found it too much and dropped out. I was alone, apart from my guide, but determined to carry on, fighting to banishing the self-doubts and fears that were looming in those dark hours before the dawn. By keeping a positive focus and silently repeating, like a mantra, 'You can do it. Never, ever, give up,' I found the inner strength to realise my ambition and reach the summit.

In many ways the journey up Mt. Kinabalu mirrored the preceding few years of my life. I was fortunate to have had great support but nobody, no matter how caring, could take away my pain or make the journey for me. It was down to me to generate the inner belief to reach where I wanted to be. The darkness slowly lifting on the mountain that morning, giving way to such a beautiful dawn, was symbolic of my personal darkness fading and gradually revealing the colour, beauty and vibrancy of life again.

In those moments of quiet contemplation at 4,095 metres I began to see that I had much to be grateful for.

Catherine Musto, Psychotherapist & Awareness Coach

ATTITUDE – BELIEF – COURAGE

I first met Sandi in 2003 when we were looking for women to sign up for the 3B Challenge – a multi-activity expedition to Jordan to raise awareness of the importance of exercise to ward off the brittle bone disease known as osteoporosis. Sandi was a newcomer to adventure travel. I still joke with her now about how she turned up at the airport for the start of the challenge wearing stilettos, bling jewellery and carrying a regular suitcase instead of the team duffle bag. She did have the team T-shirt on so all was not lost. The stilettos were soon replaced by hiking boots as we began the challenge; the earrings and necklace also came off! I advise people to expect the unexpected on adventure trips; that said, I didn't expect Sandi to break her front tooth within the first two days of the challenge (she took a fall off her bike when we were riding into Wadi Rum). In this instance, instead of focusing on the negative she focused on the positive – fabulous dental work and an amazing smile to prove it. Sandi acknowledges her weaknesses, moves on, focuses on her strengths and celebrates her success – however small or large.

Sandi had a gone through some pretty big personal challenges along her own life journey, here's what she has to share.

> *Facing the most devastating financial crisis of my life I realised I had relied too much on others to take care of me, I had taken things for granted and had honestly left the responsibility of my well-being on others. With a mountain of debts and expenses staring me in the face, panic and fear paralysed me. Confusion, palpitations, sleepless nights, job rejections and relationships going down the drain – not a good place to be!*

> *I truly believe my attitude was and is still the key to my well-being. In the state that I was I truly needed courage and confidence and that could only come from within. I sought answers from outside of myself, opinions, suggestions, and advice because I felt totally inadequate,*

incapable and unworthy enough to find out what could work for me.

I believe in the power of prayer with clear intent and that is what finally worked for me. My prayers were answered and I managed to secure a job, a job that I have held with the same company for the last 20 years – not bad for someone who, at the age of 44, had never worked a day in her life.

The adventure trips I signed up with Jules taught me so much self-reliance and at the same time acknowledging and being grateful to those around me. While I acknowledged my weaknesses I also celebrated my strengths. The trips with Jules awakened many dormant feelings in me. Today I continue to challenge myself in all spheres of my life. I have chosen to say yes to several adventure challenges through Mountain High: snake boat races in Kerala, skydiving, horseback riding in Mongolia, dog sledding in the Arctic to name a few.

Age is just a number – Attitude is what matters

Believe in YOU

Courage, conviction and confidence

That's my ABC – and most important of all LOVE yourself.

Sandi 'Rich' Saksena, Personal Finance Professional

MAPPING OUT A NEW PATH

If you have already come to a conclusion that something needs to change, you are ready to move on and want something better for yourself, it's time to start tapping into your inner mountain of resources and create a route. I like to use mind maps and find them very useful for setting out different areas that need to be worked on in order to bring a goal to fruition.

BRIGHT IDEA:

Take a large piece of paper and write your goal in the centre and circle it, then branch off from that goal and form circles all around the main goal and write all the things you need to do to bring that goal to fruition. Look back to the key resources you identified in the treasure chest exercise (your strengths) and start using these strengths to act on your goals. Realising your goals requires dedication and effort, know that YOU have all the resources inside necessary for you to make this happen.

VISUALISE YOUR SUCCESS

It was an American gymnastics tutor at school who taught me how to visualise. I was 11 years old and loved this as it allowed my vivid imagination to run free. Her name was Miss Martini (we used to call her Boozer even though we had no idea whether she actually did drink Martinis). At the beginning and end of every class she would have us close our eyes and imagine the perfect 10 routine – to put ourselves in the picture, to see, feel and hear every single movement. I loved using this technique and continue to use it now – seeing myself on top of a mountain, writing this book, having successful meetings… I love making films in my mind… and also take lots of mental holidays imagining myself on a beach, in a forest, swimming in the ocean (even though I might be stuck in traffic at the time!). Even Arnold Schwarzenegger imagined his biceps to be mountain peaks as he pumped iron in the gym!

On a psychological level, envisioning success can enhance motivation and confidence. Whether you are walking on a mountain trail or only picture it, you activate many of the same neural networks: paths of interconnected nerve cells that link what your body does to the brain impulses that control it. Mental imagery workouts stimulate the sympathetic nervous system, which governs our fight-or-flight response and causes increases in heart rate, breathing and blood pressure. So simply envisioning a movement elicits nervous system responses comparable to those recorded during physical execution of the same action. When you repeatedly imagine performing a task, you also condition your neural pathways so that the action feels familiar when you go to perform it; it's as if you're carving a groove in your nervous system. Start making your own films in your mind – with you playing the starring role. **PRESS PLAY!**

Here's a story to highlight how visualisation in action led to success.

HARRY POTTER PADDLES

In 2007 I teamed up with Gray, a dragon boat paddling coach, to train the first and only team of breast cancer survivors team from the UAE to take part in an international dragon boat race in Penang Malaysia. As well as the physical training we set up for the team, I added in mental imagery training – getting the team to imagine that their paddle had magical Harry Potter qualities so that every time the blade entered the water a massive surge of energy was created, an energy that was so powerful that it carried the boat forward three times the normal distance of one stroke. I asked the team to imagine a bright swirling force of energy swooshing through the water each time their paddle went into the water and to see our dragon boat flying through the finishing line with the UAE flag raised high. I asked them to imagine this every day leading up to the competition. After just seven weeks of training we flew to Penang ready to race. We had all envisaged a pink dragon boat to race in; to our delight, we saw one in the line-up when we got to the race venue – the dragon boat gods were with us!

When the race officials called out the teams for the race we were allocated the pink boat (ask and you shall receive!). Each of us took our position on the boat: 10 women with magical paddles in hand, Dr Houriya Kazim as drummer, and me as coxwoman steering the boat. We made our way to the start point – calm, centred and ready to press play and paddle! The start horn sounded and we were off.

With every drum beat the magical paddles entered the water bringing the finishing line closer towards us. "Go, Go, Go, Drive, Drive" – simple clear instructions from the rear as we moved away from the other five boats in the race and started catching up with the current world champions, Australia, who were three boat lengths ahead of us. Just as we had all imagined it, we felt like we were flying, there was so much energy on, in and around our boat, the dream was now a reality as we stormed through the finishing line to win silver medals, just 11 seconds behind the winning Australian team – and yes, the UAE flag was flying high!

A.U.D.R.E.Y.

Whether we are aware of it or not, we are continually contributing to the story of our life by how we think, feel, act and speak.

To enable people to get moving in all areas of their life, I created the A.U.D.R.E.Y. mastermind principle. The basic concept of A.U.D.R.E.Y. is that the moment you become aware of a situation and then start to understand it, you have the opportunity to disassociate then reprogramme/rescript it to a more emotionally charged, compelling situation that gets you to your YES or eureka moment:

A = Awareness

U = Understanding

D = Disassociation

R = Reprogramme and rescript

E = Emotionally charged

Y = YES!

For an in-depth explanation of A.U.D.R.E.Y. complete with a 30-day challenge to help you think, eat, move and sleep like a champion, go to the Jules Lewis website noted at the back of the book.

"Your answers lie inside of you. The answer to all of life's questions lies inside of you.

All you need to do is look, listen and trust."
– Cherie Carter-Scott

In the words of the song by Foreigner, *Don't stop believing,* be the bright shining star you were meant to be and know that within you lies limitless potential just waiting to be unlocked and put into action. Think about this: the Mountain in You plus the Mountain in Me equals the Mountain in US: a fabulous range of mountains in the world – stronger together. Search for the mountain within you – listen and learn from her, she is YOU. Your first duty is to be YOURSELF… and every day is a chance to SHINE like the mountain jewel you are.

"Within you there is a stillness and a sanctuary to which you can retreat any time."
– Hermann Hess

Here's some sound advice from Max Ehrmann's *Desiderata*:

"Go placidly amid the noise and the haste, and remember what peace there may be in silence. As far as possible, without surrender, be on good terms with all persons.

Speak your truth quietly and clearly; and listen to others, even to the dull and the ignorant; they too have their story.

Avoid loud and aggressive persons; they are vexatious to the spirit.

If you compare yourself with others, you may become vain or bitter, for always there will be greater and lesser persons than yourself.

Enjoy your achievements as well as your plans. Keep interested in your own career, however humble; it is a real possession in the changing fortunes of time.

Exercise caution in your business affairs, for the world is full of trickery.

But let this not blind you to what virtue there is; many persons strive for high ideals, and everywhere life is full of heroism.

Be yourself. Especially, do not feign affection. Neither be cynical about love; for in the face of all aridity and disenchantment, it is as perennial as the grass.

Take kindly the counsel of the years, gracefully surrendering the things of youth.

Nurture strength of spirit to shield you in sudden misfortune. But do not distress yourself with dark imaginings. Many fears are born of fatigue and loneliness.

Beyond a wholesome discipline, be gentle with yourself. You are a child of the universe no less than the trees and the stars; you have a right to be here.

And whether or not it is clear to you, no doubt the universe is unfolding as it should. Therefore be at peace with God, whatever you conceive Him to be.

And whatever your labors and aspirations, in the noisy confusion of life, keep peace in your soul. With all its sham, drudgery and broken dreams, it is still a beautiful world.

Be cheerful. Strive to be happy."

– Max Ehrmann

For the section below, follow the same instructions given in Chapter 1.

1. MEDITATE

2. COME TO YOUR SENSES

3. AFFIRMATION

It's all in me – I am the Mountain

4. POWER OF THREE

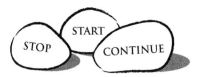

What are you going to start, stop and continue doing as a result of reading this chapter?

What's your 'IT'S ALL IN YOU' STORY?

Write it now.

What are you excited, committed and grateful for in relation to this chapter? Jot your thoughts down in your journal or on the Notes pages at the end of the book.

MOVE AND THE WAY WILL OPEN

IT'S IMPORTANT TO KNOW WHERE YOU WANT TO GO

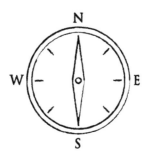

"If you don't know where you are going,
you might wind up someplace else."

– Yogi Berra

I started writing this chapter in London Heathrow airport. When you are in an airport it is very useful to know where you want to go! Just imagine the chaos if you were to turn up at the airport with no ticket and no idea where you wanted to go. You could have some fun doing it though! There is no way you would get into the car every day without knowing where you were heading; if you did you could spend a lot of time going round in circles, drifting aimlessly, and getting nowhere fast – very frustrating and a waste of your precious time, unless of course you have plenty of time to spare.

The clearer you are about where you want to go and how you plan to get there, the greater your chances of success.

HEADING IN THE RIGHT DIRECTION

Knowing exactly what I want to do and where I want to go plays a big part in my life and work – I am sure it does for you too. It's fair to say I would be out of business pretty quickly if I left such decisions to chance.

For every expedition, retreat, workshop or presentation I intend to run I create vision boards and mind maps to build on and refer to right up until delivery time. Having organised and led multinational teams of women and men on over 55 expeditions to more than 20 countries, it's important for me to know how to get to where we want to go and do everything possible to make sure we get there – in time, on time, taking the best route for the team's success – and being able to course-correct if and when necessary. Even with good planning in place sometimes things don't go to plan – so make sure you have a plan B and C… all the way to Z if needs be!

"If you do not change direction,
you may end up where you are heading."

– Lao Tzu

BRIGHT IDEA:

You can do this exercise now or after you have read this chapter – in fact do it any time you want to get clear in where you want to go! This is easy and fun! Decide on where you want to go on your next holiday and create a vision board for the trip using images of all the places you want to see, the activities you want to do, the places you want to stay. This will save you heaps of time when you arrive because you'll already know exactly where you want to go. Make sure you leave some open space on your board for something unplanned to drop in – life is full of surprises so leave some space for them!

THE WANDERER

I am now going to offer you the flip side of the coin! As much as I am all for planning ahead and knowing where you want to go, it's also great fun to just go with the flow and see where your walk or drive takes you. This works when time and getting to a particular place is not important; take time out to have fun just cruising or wandering around with the sole purpose of being open to whatever shows up. It's amazing what you find when you go off the beaten track and create some trails of your own. Let me know any great finds please!

"When you come to a fork in the road, take it."

– Yogi Berra

KNOWING WHAT YOU WANT

If you put something in your mouth and it tastes awful, more often than not you will spit it out. If you turn the radio on and the type of music playing is not to your liking, you will change channels or switch it off. If you go into a room and it smells like rotten eggs, you will walk out. By choosing to move away from what you don't want you can then course-correct and make new choices to move you towards what you do want.

How often do you choose comfort over change: going to the same places, hanging out with the same people, doing the same things, eating the same food, having the same conversations, staying in a relationship that's really going nowhere, staying in a job or in a place that's not fulfilling, watching a crappy film thinking that it will get better then reaching the end and wondering why on earth you stayed? Do you keep doing the same things and expect something different to happen? What needs to change? The longer you drift without purpose and direction, the more lost you can become. It's easy to drift along more out of habit than a clear direction; think about what habits you would like to change that would shift you to where you really want to go.

IF YOU DON'T LIKE WHERE YOU ARE – MOVE!

Eric, the taxi driver who took me to Madison airport, was a perfect example of the magic that happens when you choose to move. He was not happy living in New Canaan, yet still kept putting off the move to Madison where a friend had suggested he would feel more at home. He went back and forth to visit and really enjoyed his time there. After two years it finally sunk in: instead of visiting why not move there – after all, that's where he felt so much more at home. He packed up, made the move, met the woman of his dreams and is so much happier – if you don't like where you are, MOVE!

INNER COMPASS

Have you ever noticed how many people ignore the directions of their inner compass and wonder why they don't end up where they want to be? What about you? Have you traded your real passion for comfort and routine? Do you make the same choices day in day out, more out of habit than a clear direction? Are you drifting through life or are you in the driving seat? I know it's easy to stay in one place – especially when you have been knocked off your feet and need time to reassess before you make any major moves. In 1998 my husband of seven years, a professional squash player, literally dropped dead with a heart aneurism at the age of 41 after a squash match. This was totally unexpected and meant a massive change in my personal circumstances. He was gone forever and I was left to deal with the aftermath of a sudden death in a foreign country as well as the loss and emotions I was experiencing.

All of a sudden I found myself in the depths of a dark valley, the only way to move up and out of it was to focus on all the practical things that needed to be sorted, get help where I needed it, keep looking up, moving forward, resting when I needed to and digging deep for the strength and resilience to see me through. I could write a whole book on this alone, but that is not the purpose of this book. This book shares how you can get back up when you have been knocked down or are feeling stuck in some way. I chose to turn the painful experience of loss to a burning desire to inspire others to reach new personal and professional heights. My wish is that what you read in the book will help you get up and moving again – and inspire you to climb a mountain!

After the shock of what had happened sunk in, it was clear I had two choices: go down with him or focus on what I could do to lift myself back up. I was still alive, no longer a wife, yet still a daughter, a sister, a friend – still me and still lots of things to sort out and deal with before I could get moving again. At the time I had read and been advised that making any big changes after the death of a loved one was not smart; it made a lot of sense at the time so I chose to stay where I was, to stay in the same job, live in the same apartment, stick to the same daily routine, as if nothing had happened. A whole year passed by and most of the things and people that needed taking care of on a practical level were complete. Now the focus had come full circle back to me: what direction was I going to take next? It was a scary question. It would have been very easy to 'keep on keeping on' but this no longer felt right for me, I felt I needed to go on a journey – and go alone.

One morning I looked at myself in the mirror as I was brushing my teeth, I got close up so I could see deep into my eyes and asked: What are you afraid of, what happened to your warrior spirit, the one that gave you the courage to leave Yorkshire and work in Kuwait in 1989 instead of staying with all your friends and family? Where is the woman who escaped across the desert when Iraq invaded Kuwait, the woman who was not afraid to move? The answer was clear: I had slipped into auto-pilot cruise mode and stayed a little too long for my liking. I would not go as far as to say I was fast asleep by the roadside while life passed me by, however my *joie de vivre* had gone missing in action and I wanted it back!

At the time, the Men at Work song *Living in the Land Down Under* had been playing on the radio almost every hour. Lynne, the personnel manager at the hotel and beach resort where I was working at the time had recently moved to Australia to start a new life. We had kept in touch and she had said that I was welcome to visit anytime so I decided to take her up on the offer! I bought a copy of the *Lonely Planet* guide on Australia and started making plans. Seven weeks later I had stepped down from my job, packed up the apartment, had a plan in place and was on a plane heading to Sydney. Strewth, I was really going 'walkabout'. No phone, just a Hotmail account set up to send reassuring messages to my family in the UK (who I must say were all rather concerned that I was wandering around Australia).

Lynne met me at Sydney airport and I spent three days with her in Cronulla, New South Wales before really going walkabout. If you are planning a big trip after a significant emotional experience it does help to know at least one person in the country you intend to go walkabout in. Even if you have no intention of spending little or any time with them, it's just smart to have a point of contact if for any reason you need some help. So, I knew exactly where I wanted to go and what I wanted to see, yet was also open to being sidetracked. I spent two months exploring, ticking off my *Lonely Planet* list – the ultimate tourist. During my visit I did my open water dive course (this opened up a whole new world), had two drumming lessons, made new friends, taught a few aerobic classes at a local sports club, went to the zoo (I love kangaroos and koalas) and spent days in the Blue Mountains – and I didn't feel blue, in fact I was starting to feel more alive than I had felt in a long time.

I loved the time I spent at the beach, wiggling my toes in the sand and allowing the sun and wind to revitalise my spirit. I swam in the sea (no sharks in sight) and really started to let go of a lot of thoughts, feelings and emotions that had been weighing me down – letting them wash away into the ocean. I took time to journal and start thinking about what I wanted to do next on the career front – it was time for a change from the sports industry. My life had changed and it was time for a change. By leaving everything I knew behind I allowed myself time and space to think about the next chapter of my life, and where I wanted to go. Time for a comeback!

"When the pain of being the same becomes greater than the pain of being different, you change."

– Deepak Chopra

WAKE-UP CALLS

Sometimes someone or something is the catalyst for personal or professional change; it could be the end or beginning of a relationship, the death or birth of a loved one, the loss of a job, a posting overseas or a major health challenge. It could be a book or a film that you see that triggers a shift in your mindset; a conversation with someone that rocks your world and beckons you to a new one.

Sometimes you have your own wake-up call as I did that one morning back in 1999. All of a sudden the fog lifts and you can see and sense what you need to do to shift from living in auto-pilot to truly being in the now, wide awake to your situation – to what needs to change. The dots start to connect, the universe sends you signs almost every day now, your gut feelings get stronger and stronger, the voice in your head gets louder and louder, your intuition and internal compass guide you to make new choices – and you know you have to get moving.

MOVING ON AT LOW POINTS OF YOUR LIFE

When I first moved to Dubai in 1997 I joined the International Business Women's Group and met so many incredible women from very diverse backgrounds who had all carved out a full life for themselves. One of the women I met, Tricia, was an inspiration to so many of us, little did I know at the time just how much she had gone through.

This is Tricia's story about how she got moving at a very low point in her life.

I had an IVF baby in October 1997 as an older mum of 41. My beloved dad died in January 1998, and then my husband (who I'd thought was my soul mate) announced that he was leaving in March 1998, leaving me as a single parent of a five-month-old baby daughter in Dubai – so it was a real emotional roller coaster five months for me, on top of a roller coaster year-long IVF process! My first reaction at my husband reneging on our life together was complete surprise and disbelief.

The one thing I knew instinctively was that I needed to take as much pressure off myself as possible, as I was in no fit state to make big life decisions in the immediate aftermath. So first of all I got my support network in place (a few close friends who I could vent to, a dependable housekeeper who kept things clean and sorted at home, my mum who was my rock and 'life support' for me and my daughter, and a great PA) and importantly I gave myself time and permission to grieve/rant/scream/vent as much as I needed to... and I sure needed to!

The shock came in waves as I realised that this was it. I had to make a few key decisions for how I wanted my life to be from here on. So I started to write down what I definitely DIDN'T want in my life, and then what I DID want started to emerge loud and clear. The very act of writing things down enabled me to push my emotions to one side and make decisions based on facts.

I already had a business established in Dubai and was financially able to support myself (an important factor in the decision process). It was a lot easier to be a single mum in Dubai than in the UK because of the easy access to household help. It was extremely important to me that it was me who raised our daughter, not a nanny or a housekeeper. Dubai was a very family-friendly place to raise a child.

So I made the decision to stay in Dubai, run my business part-time from home so I was around for my daughter and could revel in raising her and to delegate EVERYTHING possible to my housekeeper and PA. The other thing I did which was a great decision was to use some of my savings to pay my rent for two years in advance, and that took a huge amount of financial pressure off me until I was feeling able to step up the level of my business. So I created a platform for myself that enabled me to thrive and move forwards fast!

Fast forward 18 years and my daughter Sian and I have had a wonderful life together. Getting the support I needed in place and taking pressure off myself in those early days were key in making it work and keeping me 'whole'. It was so important for me to be very clear on how I wanted to things to work out, to have a clear direction and go for it.

Tricia Evans, Business Coach

FEEDING YOUR MIND WITH KINDER THOUGHTS

Over the last few years I have been going back and forth to Qatar to deliver talks on stress management, emotional resilience and peak performance. On one of my visits I had the opportunity to meet Liz Keaney who certainly learnt the hard way when it comes to wake-up calls. By changing her inner thoughts, words and intentions she found life started to unfold in exactly the right direction.

What if the 'thing' that has prevented you from getting all you want in life – your vitality, joy and abundance – is not something outside of you? What if that thing is inside of you – your voice! You know the one, the one that speaks unkindly to you, all day every day. The little voice that says you're too old, too young, too fat, too skinny, too qualified, not qualified enough... the one that constantly puts you down, distracts you from getting moving and stepping into your own greatness.

Everything changed for me the day I realised that two cancer diagnoses in 12 months was a wake-up call. Time to wake up and listen, have an awareness of my inner voice and my habitual self-talk. It was time to recognise how I could feed my mind with kinder thoughts to help my health as well as my happiness, wealth and inner peace. The day I made myself worthy of the 'seeds' of self-kindness with my thoughts, words and intentions everything started to unfold magnificently, in exactly the right direction.

Liz Keaney, author of Warrior Women

WHEN THINGS ARE NOT GOING RIGHT – GO LEFT!

Every choice that you make has the power to alter the direction of your life – pretty big statement I know. The quality of your choices dictate whether you will stay stuck, struggle or live the life of your dreams. What will you choose?

You are free to choose to move forward, left, right, or backwards, to be happy or sad, single or married, set up your own business or work for others, move overseas or stay in your home country, have children or not have children. You can also choose to not choose for a while, although when you do this you are in danger of letting life make some choices for you and then you wonder what happened... instead of making things happen.

Your choices can fill you with pleasure or fill you with pain. You don't wake up one morning and find you are 3kg heavier, it happens over a period of time due to the daily choices you have made. The good news is that you and you alone have the choice to change anything in your life at any moment. When you want something enough you will do whatever it takes to find a way to make it happen. I know that sometimes your choices need to be backed up by the financial ability to follow through with them, so work on getting a plan in place that allows you to keep moving forward. You might also have to take into consideration your family commitments and how any changes you are planning to make will impact them. Many of the choices that can positively impact your life are small and within your reach; your big dreams shape your reality yet it is the small daily consistent choices that move you closer to your dreams.

New choices lead to new actions and new actions lead to new results. If you sense you are not on the right path – GET OFF IT OR TAKE A VERY SHARP LEFT!

LIFE'S DRIVING FORCE – VALUES

When you find yourself stuck and struggling with what to do next or where you want to go, re-examining your core values is a really good start. I see values as a set of waypoints on your inner compass that guide and keep you on track whatever else is going on around you. Values are your directional driving force that will take you from where you are now to where you want to be.

Our choices are a reflection of our values. When you look at your life as it is now it is a reflection of your choices in the past. The good news is it's never too late to make new choices and re-set your internal compass.

There are lots of great books on values; my favourite one just happens to be written by a very dear friend, Jo Simpson, author of *The Restless Executive: Reclaim Your Values, Love What You Do and Lead with Purpose.* I highly recommend you pick up a copy.

In the meantime I will keep this short and simple, in a nutshell:

Values…

- Determine how you spend your time

- Who you spend your time with

- What you spend your money on

- What you commit yourself to

- How you live your life

- How you fill your space

- Reflect on your internal dialogue, affirmations and conversations with others

Our values are simply those things that are most important to us and at the very core of who we believe ourselves to be. When we know our values, we can live a happier life doing what's most important to us and ultimately positively impact those around us. They are critical to accomplishing great things in your life and will help you map out a deliberate plan for your future.

Whenever you find yourself in a transitional period in your life – and believe me there will be lots of them – it's a good idea to check in with your core values to see if they are still fully aligned with your new circumstances.

FINDING YOUR WAY

In the summer of 2015, 18 of us walked the last 111km of the Camino De Santiago from Sarria (in north-west Spain) to Santiago De Compostela. The route is also known as 'The Way'. You may have read Paulo Coelho's book *The Pilgrimage* or seen the film with Martin Sheen entitled *The Way*, in which case you will really relate to this part of the book. There are many start points for the route (France, Portugal, Spain); however, one thing is common all along the way: the yellow arrows that mark out the route and make it possible to find your way to the end point – Santiago De Compostela. The yellow arrows could easily represent your core values; by following and aligning with them you will always find a way to make it to where you want to go. I highly recommend you take time out to walk the Camino – ideally the whole way which takes about a month, something my husband Calin and I intend to do. Our guide for the 2015 trip, Santiago Garcia, was totally passionate about the history and the religious and spiritual essence of the walk. In his own way he recognised that the walk mirrors life in so many ways.

> *Walking the Camino means the effort to reach a goal that means something to you. You are putting yourself to some effort that resembles life's ups and downs: easy paths,*

rocky paths, good weather, bad weather... just like life's path where whatever is going on around us you connect to what matters most and encourage yourselves onwards, supporting the people around you with a smile, a 'Buen camino' or extending a hand to help the next step.

The benefit from doing the Camino is not walking the Camino, but to walk inside yourself and go through your memories and remember things that you don't have the chance in the regular day-to-day, because living in a city stresses or obliges you to follow a certain routine. On the Camino, you follow the yellow arrows to guide you, yet you set the internal path and take your time to explore your thoughts, to think about actions, suffering, achievements and how you can bring the best of you to every single day. Despite the blisters, every day you finish each stage with a big smile and a tremendous feeling of achievement. This is what you learn along the Camino, that your goals are all reachable if you persevere and keep on walking.

Along the Camino I walk, learn, listen, make effort, express feelings, love, appreciate, value, grow, walk, analyse, reflect and many other things in one, this is the Camino, the way to purify yourself and your soul as you find your Way.

Santiago Garcia, GM Iberia

CLARITY

Clarity on your values and taking consistent daily action that aligns with them truly sets you free to enjoy the journey. When you are clear on your values the answers to the questions below are so much easier; your job is to make sure that every move and decision you make aligns with your core values.

BRIGHT IDEA:

Stop reading and grab a pen and your journal and answer the following questions in relation to specific areas of your life that you would like to make some changes in (health, career, finances, relationships).

- What's the situation now?

- What changes would you like to make?

- List the top three core values that will be your guiding lights and driving force during this transition.

- What three things can you do daily to move you towards your goal?

TOWARDS OR AWAY

Simple advice: every time you have to make a choice or a decision, ask yourself: Will this choice help me move towards my goal or keep me away from my goal? If the answer is yes then go for it. If it is no then don't do it! Learn to say no so you can say yes to yourself. Instead of thinking "I should do this", move your thinking and change your words to "I have decided to, or I choose to do this" as it reflects and reinforces that it is your choice.

Choices have the power to impact your life. If you want your life to be different you have to make different choices. From my own experience I know that making new choices can be uncomfortable yet it's the only way to get you moving towards an inspired future instead of staying stuck, safe, or, worse still, heading in the wrong direction. I chose to leave the security of a full-time job to start Mountain High. I have turned projects away so I can focus on the ones that are more important to me. I chose to sign up to organisations that move me towards my goals, for example joining the NSA (National Speakers Association). When I buy things, sign up for courses, decide on what to eat or which events to go to it really does help to ask, "will this move me towards my goals or away from them?" Simple example, if your goal is to lose weight the next time you are looking at a big piece of triple chocolate fudge cake you might choose to think twice.

COMMITMENT

A constant never-ending commitment to what you want to do and where you want to go is the main ingredient that separates the ordinary from the extraordinary. Anything that is truly important to you in life and aligns with your values is worthy of your full commitment – here's a quote on commitment that I really like:

"Until one is committed, there is hesitancy, a chance to draw back… there is one elementary truth, the ignorance of which kills countless ideas and splendid plans; that the moment one commits, the providence moves too. All sorts of things occur to help one that would never have occurred… incidents, meetings and material assistance which no man could have dreamed of would come his way."

– Goethe

By the way, I have found that whenever I have committed to something 100% lots of good things have happened. A quick example was when I committed to take a professional videographer on a Polar expedition, not knowing where the cash to cover her costs would come from. Within 24 hours of committing we had a call from a sponsor to say they would cover filming costs – awesome!

What are you going to commit to today?

CRYSTAL CLEAR

 ## BRIGHT IDEA:

Stop reading for a moment and take hold of the clear quartz crystal I asked you to get at the start of the book (if you didn't manage to find one use anything that represents clarity to you), hold it in your left hand (left hand is for receiving), close your eyes and visualise what you want to do, where you want to go, who you want to be, what you want to have. Put yourself in the picture and see, feel and hear everything.

When you have finished this exercise, open your eyes, pick up your journal and pen and write down whatever you have seen; better still, create a vision board* that replicates what you have created in your mind. Look at it every day and remind yourself why this is so important to you, your family, your team, or your business.

In addition to vision boards I use post-it notes with embedded positive suggestions to keep me on track. I place these on the fridge, bathroom mirror, office noticeboard, on the dashboard of the car and in my wallet as constant reminders: something as simple as Drink More Water – Go the Gym – Call five potential sponsors – You are gorgeous – Write your book!!!!

* Vision boards are simply boards that you can create with images, symbols, mantras, quotes that represent everything you would like to bring into your life and are inspired by.

CONTRAST TO CLARITY

When I work with clients who say, "I don't really know what I want," I ask, "What is it that you don't want in relation to this area of your life?" Believe it or not this works a treat. For some people writing down a list of what they don't want in relation to a specific area of their life allows them to identify what they do want – this is opposition thinking at its best. So, for example, knowing that you don't want to work full-time highlights that you prefer to work part-time or on a contract basis. Knowing that you don't like working on your own indicates that you prefer to work with a team. By listing out what you don't want it becomes very easy to write the exact opposite of what you don't want and end up with a clear list of what you do want. I wrote a list of all the things I was looking for in a man and two months later he appeared! I write lists of countries I want to visit, mountains I want to climb, and one by one they get ticked off the list. Get clear on what you want – write it down – create a vision board – post your commands where you can see them – and get moving!

LAND ROVER

When I first started Mountain High in November 2003 I moved out of my own apartment into shared beach villa accommodation; I knew where I wanted to go with my business and paying expensive rent was not on the list! When I stepped down from my previous job I had to hand back the company car so I rented a Mitsubishi Lancer for a while. On my Mountain High vision board I had a picture of a silver Land Rover on it. A 4x4 that would allow me to take clients across sand, rock, mud – and carry kayaks on the roof and bikes on the back! I set my intentions and believed that one day I would have a silver Land Rover. In December 2003 I set up a meeting with Land Rover at their regional office in Dubai to discuss sponsoring a project in Jordan we were working on: a multi-activity adventure challenge for 24 women to highlight the importance of exercise to prevent osteoporosis. We needed cars to move around in Jordan as we completed several challenges (hiking, biking, kayaking, canyoning, tandem skydives to name a few!). Jannike joined me for the meeting as we were working on this together. The meeting went well; Wouter (the Land Rover communications manager at the time) was blown away by the mind map of the challenge I had created – he even asked to photocopy it!). We asked for exactly what we wanted: two promotional Land Rovers for us to use in Dubai and eight Land Rovers in Jordan for the team. He said he would get back to us within a couple of weeks.

A day later I left for Jordan to plan out the trip with my ground handlers; when I came back Land Rover confirmed their sponsorship. Jannike and I were given two branded LR2s to drive around Dubai to promote the challenge. The challenge team of 24 women were also able to experience a Land Rover training day with Wouter before we left for the challenge, and to top it all, we had eight Land Rovers waiting for us in Jordan. We managed to secure great coverage of our challenge, leading to US$300,000 of media exposure for our campaign. We also secured HRH Queen Rania of Jordan as our Patron as at the time she was the Chairwoman of the International Osteoporosis Foundation.

When we came back from the trip we had to give the two promotional Land Rovers back, so it was back to a hire car for me – at least for a little while! I looked at my vision board every day and totally believed that the silver Land Rover was on its way. A few weeks later I asked for a meeting with the marketing team at Land Rover armed with lots of plans for more expeditions and suggested that they might like to sponsor me with a Land Rover for the year (for as many years as possible, please!). Besides, what a great way to highlight their brand: adventure – discovery – women in action – in the driving seat, practically perfect match! To cut a very long story short, I was called back into the offices to sign off a sponsorship agreement that included cash for projects and a brand spanking new LR3. When I saw it in the car park I couldn't stop smiling – it was silver!!! I remember sitting in it and pinching myself, this is for real… happy tears and a very big smile on my face as I drove out of the car park, my head swimming with ideas to put this amazing new vehicle to work.

It's important to know what you want and where you want to go!

Are you wandering through life or are you in the driver's seat heading exactly where you want to go?

Time to switch off again… you know the routine now.

1. MEDITATE

2. COME TO YOUR SENSES

3. AFFIRMATION
I am on my Chosen Path and Heading in the Right Direction

4. POWER OF THREE

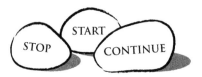

What are you going to start, stop and continue doing as a result of reading this chapter?

What's your 'IT'S IMPORTANT TO KNOW WHERE YOU WANT TO GO' STORY?

Write it now.

What are you excited, committed and grateful for in relation to this chapter? Jot your thoughts down in your journal or on the Notes pages at the end of the book.

WHAT'S
STOPPING YOU?

CHAPTER 4

TAKING ACTION BUILDS COURAGE AND CONFIDENCE

"Often we are caught in a mental trap of seeing enormously successful people and thinking they are where they are because they have some special gift. Yet a closer look shows that the greatest gift that extraordinarily successful people have over the average person is their ability to get themselves to take action."

– Tony Robbins

CULTIVATE A BIAS FOR ACTION

If I had to suggest one quality that will increase the chance of success more than anything else, it would be the ability to take action. Action is the key to success. In my quest for knowledge and personal growth I have taken part in many workshops and seminars in several fields that interest me. Knowledge is power; however, I have learnt that taking action on any knowledge gained is so much more powerful. Knowledge that stays in your head with no action attached to it provides zero benefit, so ACT on what you have learnt as soon as possible and teach it to others – it's a great way to reinforce your learning!

If you are serious about being successful, and I trust that you are, never let a single day go by without taking action – however small it is. When you have a vision in your head about where you would like to be in the future and what you would like to be doing it will require action. The minute you apply massive action to your knowledge, it has a faster and greater impact on your life.

"You can have many great ideas in your head, but what makes the difference is the action. Without action upon an idea, there will be no manifestation, no results, and no reward."

– Miguel Ruiz

WHEN – THEN – SHOULD – COULD

Sometimes we choose to wait for conditions to be perfect to take action. The 'when… then' approach can keep you stuck. 'When I have more time or money then I will…' 'When I have done more training courses then I will…' What are your 'when… then' excuses? When you hear yourself saying I should have done, or I could have done, these are words of warning that no action or the wrong action was taken.

The longer an idea sits in your head without being acted upon, the weaker it tends to become. Other ideas and life situations can easily get in the way of your original idea. Every action you take builds more and more momentum and takes you closer to making the idea a reality. If you don't take action on an idea someone else will; how many times have you had a great idea, not acted upon it, and then seen someone else put that same or similar idea into action? Painful isn't it?!

"Any action is better than no action, especially if you have been in an unhappy situation for a long time."
— Eckhart Tolle

BRIGHT IDEA:

Keep an ideas list in your journal, highlight the ones that resonate most with you and are aligned with your values. Choose one and take three actions that will help you move forward on this idea – do this every day until you have reached your goal. Repeat on all your highlighted ideas.

WHAT'S NOW

Getting organised and focusing on what you can do right now is key to success. Let go of any worry about what you should have done last week or what you need to do tomorrow, focus only on what needs to be done right NOW. If you think too much about the past or the future it drains your energy and distracts you from what needs to be done at the moment. Lighten your load and focus on what matters most… NOW. ASK YOURSELF: "WHAT ONE STEP CAN I TAKE RIGHT NOW TO MOVE THINGS FORWARD?" You can and will break free from "analysis paralysis" and feeling stuck by taking the smallest of actions; it doesn't always need to be a quantum leap to make a difference. If you still don't have an answer think of someone who could shift your thinking. Phone a friend, ask for help, or read a book on the subject that is challenging you. Instead of lying awake in bed at night or sitting on the couch of doubt and worry get up, get out, and get walking and talking. Small steps can and do make a big difference, make the first move and the way will open.

ACCOUNTABILITY

As a curious solo entrepreneur with an interest in many different things, I know how easy it is to get distracted. It takes courage and discipline to do what needs to be done on a daily basis, to be a self-starter rather than waiting for someone else to tell you what to do. I have learnt that accountability to someone or something will help you keep on track – a daily, weekly, monthly check in with someone who can keep you on your toes and moving forward.

We all need a gentle nudge or wake-up call conversation from time to time. Working with a personal trainer, coach or mentor keeps you accountable. Choose someone who has your best interests at heart; someone who will be your raving fan and offer wise, constructive, challenging counsel. Just knowing someone cares as much as you do makes a big difference. A simple "by whom" or "by when" chart that one or two other people know about keeps me accountable on projects. Having a soundboard is useful. It can be someone to highlight your blind spots, kick your butt, be your cheerleader or help you navigate through a challenge. You could argue against finding someone to be accountable to out of concern that they might replicate or imitate your ideas or, worse still, not keep your project confidential despite being asked to do so. Some people choose not to be accountable for fear of success or of being too easily influenced by other people's opinions. To make myself more accountable with day-to-day spending I now keep a daily logbook to record every single purchase I make. You can do this with food if you want to keep an eye on what you actually eat every day. I am also accountable for 10,000 steps daily to my Fitbit!

I enjoy being an accountability coach for clients, friends and family. A simple call to ask, "how are you doing with your book, diet or project?" makes all the difference.

WHO AND WHAT DO YOU NEED?

When you are choosing an accountability partner think about what kind of support you need the most, it may well be that you actually need a few people to guide you along. You may need some or all of these:

- Feedback/constructive criticism

- A confidence boost

- Someone to partner up with on a project

- A shoulder to cry on!

- Connections to people or resources

- Someone to help you lighten up and have a good laugh

- Someone to encourage you to try something new and out of your comfort zone

- Someone with a specialist skill

- Someone to help you develop and execute a strategy

WHO IS WILLING TO HOLD YOUR HAND WHEN YOU NEED IT THE MOST?

As well as being self-reliant (think back to Chapter 2 and your inner resources) I highly recommend having a diverse circle of people to reach out to and for them to know that you are happy to return the support. There is always someone who knows something or somebody you need to know to help you keep moving forward – six degrees of separation. That said, even with the best support you are the one who needs to take the action; it doesn't have to be the perfect action, the key is to do something that will bring you closer to your goal and keep moving you forward. Anything and everything is possible.

"Nothing is impossible, the word itself says I'm possible."
— Audrey Hepburn

BRIGHT IDEA:

Stop reading for a moment and think about a project you are working on or plan to start. Think about who would make a good accountability partner for you and give them a call to ask for their support. Most people enjoy helping others so expect a yes! Fix a time to connect each week and stick to it till the job is done.

BOLD ACTION REWARDED

Fortune favours the brave! After the Everest Women's Challenge in May of 2003 I came back to Dubai and asked the owner of the company I worked for if I could focus on running overseas expeditions instead of inbound tourism. His answer was a resounding no. I thought about this for a while and suggested that it was better that I stepped down from my post as my heart was set on leading team expeditions and seeing more of the world. I offered to work my notice and find a replacement – it was after all a great job and I knew someone would snap it up. I must say he did not take it very well: he asked me to pack up my desk and leave there and then – no handover to my colleagues – no cake – no handshakes and the possibility of being banned from working in the UAE… whoops! We agreed to have a cooling-off period and I took a quick break to the UK and trusted that by the time I got back things would have calmed down – thankfully they did! Now I had to take some serious action and get going! It seems the universe was happy to reward my bold action as a few days later I got chatting to a couple on a boat trip who had a travel company and they were happy to have me set up Mountain High as the adventure division under their licence giving me the opportunity to get going in record time. Within days I had my own desk, phone, business cards and a Mountain High bank account – THANK YOU, THANK YOU, THANK YOU Jeanette Peck and Paul Widger – you gave me the start I really needed!

THE COACHING COUCH

In between all the madness of leaving my job and getting started with Mountain High, I had several discussions with Tricia, a business coach based in Dubai. She worked mainly from her home office and more often than not we would sit on what I now call 'the coaching couch' – a sofa in her living room that has witnessed many long conversations. A couple of hours of guidance from Tricia on a regular basis helped me through the start-up phase of Mountain High. Having run her own business for many years, she was a great accountability partner. The wonderful thing about this is that 10 years later Tricia opened up her villa for Mountain High's 10th anniversary party in 2013 and to this day I know that I can call her any time for advice.

FEEDBACK IS THE BREAKFAST OF CHAMPIONS

As well as finding an accountability partner and taking massive action I highly recommend you have a 'go to' list of people you can call on when you are looking for open and honest feedback on how to make what you are doing or working on even better. After every trip, retreat or workshop I send out a questionnaire and use the feedback to gauge what improvements to make the next time round: what to do more of, less of, or indeed, keep exactly the same. By connecting with the people who are the most likely to book and refer your services you are tapping into their collective wisdom; this is priceless and allows you to keep taking more courageous and confident action on the path to success.

ASKING FOR HELP IS A SIGN OF STRENGTH NOT OF WEAKNESS

Think about asking a child or someone 10-20 years older than you and get their take on the situation; sometimes we get so stuck in our own mind we need to tap into someone else's to really expand our thinking. When you are stressed, unsure, going through a transition, or feeling overwhelmed, common sense rarely prevails. If after consulting your own inner wisdom you are still no closer to an answer, reach out to your circle and ask for help. Asking for help is a sign of strength, not of weakness. The saying goes that you become the average of the five people you spend the most time with, so choose wisely. The other advice I have heard is that if you are the smartest in the group of people you hang out with it's time to join another group to step up and challenge yourself more. I know when I left my job to start Mountain High the transition from being part of a team to working for myself meant I spent a lot more time alone. Thankfully I love my own company, however it soon became very obvious that teaming up with other people on specific projects was a much healthier solution and allowed me to do so much more than I could ever do alone – FIND YOUR TRIBE!

"If you want to go fast, go alone.
If you want to go further, go together."
– Kofi Annan, Global Citizen Forum

THE DISTANCE BETWEEN YOUR DREAMS AND REALITY IS CALLED ACTION

BRIGHT IDEA:

Stop reading now and grab a pen and your journal and create your 'go to' list – the names of the people who you can call on for the specific support you need. List the questions you need the answers to, identify the best person to help you, make the phone call, send the email and keep taking action until you have the answers.

NO ACTION – NO SATISFACTION

PRACTICE – PRACTICE – PRACTICE

Want to get better at taking action? Just like riding a bike, negotiating a contract, or being a parent, you'll get better at it the more you do it! Most new things involve a certain amount of discomfort so accept that you won't be brilliant at something the first time you try it. We all have our first day at work, at a sport, or maybe adjusting to a new family dynamic, so acknowledge the 'it's my first time' feeling. The more action you take, the more outcomes and results you will experience. If you do nothing, nothing changes; Sir Isaac Newton's principle states 'a body at rest tends to remain at rest and a body in motion tends to remain in motion'. It's a natural law that if you do nothing, nothing will happen; if you take minimum action the results will be minimal; if you take massive action you will get massive results. Successful people know that the major key to success is TAKING MASSIVE ACTION.

WHAT'S STOPPNG YOU?

I believe the answer to this question comes down to many things, the major ones being fear and a lack of belief. Along with your values, your belief system is the driving force behind your behaviours and your results. By changing the beliefs that constrain you in any way (limiting beliefs) you will change your behaviours. When you change your behaviours, your actions and results change. In a nutshell, your beliefs, thoughts and feelings have a massive impact on the action you take and the results you experience.

"The thing always happens that you believe in; and the belief in a thing makes it happen."

– Frank Lloyd Wright

Limiting beliefs are those that constrain you in some way, just by believing in them you rob yourself of so many opportunities. "I can't do X… because of Y, I am too old, too young, not fit enough, don't have enough experience, can't leave my family, my work, I will be judged, don't have enough qualifications, enough money, I'm useless in relationships…" The list goes on. Any of them sound familiar?

When I decided to climb a mountain for my 40th birthday a few people suggested it was a bit late to start climbing mountains, how rude and limiting of them! I often have clients call and express their concern about being in their forties and not wanting to be the granny or grandpa on a trip, retreat, or course. When I tell them I am in my fifties and have clients in their sixties who climb mountains and go dog sledding in the Arctic they soon change their limiting beliefs to more empowering ones. Think about age as being the number of years of wisdom you have accumulated rather than a barrier to your success.

If you believe that falling in love will result in being heartbroken you rob yourself from finding a soul mate. If you believe that one rejection means you will never find the right job, the right partner, the right investor, it's time to form new empowering beliefs. I use the SWSWSWSW principle whenever I experience a rejection. In short it means: some will, some won't, so what, someone else is waiting. Often rejection is simply a sign that you are barking up the wrong tree, something better is on its way or you need to adjust your strategy. You can detect limiting beliefs by listening to your self-talk. If you find the conversation in your head goes something like, "I can't do this because I am useless at sport" it's clear you have a limiting belief around your abilities in sport. The only way to shatter it is to start playing a sport and build up your confidence and skill set. I had a limiting belief around being able to hit a golf ball with a wood instead of my usual 3 iron. A lesson with a pro and lots of practice at the driving range enabled me to convert to a wood and drive the ball a good 150 yards – yay! Start to believe that you create your own reality and are responsible for what you create. The past does not equal the future and wherever there is a will there is always a way. If you are feeling confused know that you are about to learn something; while ever you are breathing you have a chance to do something great!

LIFE BEGINS AT THE END OF YOUR COMFORT ZONE

To grow and evolve as a human being (highly recommended!) and transform the ordinary into the extraordinary, more often than not it means stepping out of your comfort zone. Successful people are the ones who develop the ability to be comfortable being uncomfortable, they know that this is where the magic happens. Your comfort zone is any type of behaviour that keeps you at a steady low anxiety level. Think about something you do all the time, like brushing your teeth, commuting to work, reading the paper, watching the news. These are all everyday activities that you're used to so they won't make you feel anxious and uneasy, they are part of your comfort zone. Every time you push past first-time nerves, you build your inner strength.

When mixed with the feeling of success, a little anxiety and self-doubt actually leads to personal growth. This is why adventures like mountain climbing, white water rafting or skydiving can be so exhilarating: they induce anxiety and unease but when completed, they give you a huge feeling of accomplishment and increase your base levels of confidence. You may well discover a hidden talent in the process – the fact is, you'll never know if you don't give it a go. There's not much growth in the comfort zone, and not much comfort in the growth zone. To keep growing what can you try today to take you out of your comfort zone?

WHAT CAN YOU DO TO UTTERLY AMAZE YOURSELF?

In 2012 I organised an expedition to Antarctica and put a call out for breast cancer survivors to sign up. At the time everyone thought I was nuts and advised me that I would never find a team of women who had gone through breast cancer willing to go to the ends of the earth. How wrong they were. Within a few months of putting the word out we had a team of 12 women ready, willing and able to be roving ambassadors; to highlight the strength and spirit of women and reinforce that breast cancer is not a death sentence. The team made modern day adventure history by being the first and only multinational team of breast cancer survivors to go to Antarctica. We created a film and book on the expedition and I can hold my hand on my heart when I say this trip was AMAZING. I was totally in awe at the strength and spirit of the women on the trip and would love to share a few quotes from them as I feel sure that their words of wisdom will inspire you to keep taking action whatever life brings your way.

Don't be afraid to step out of your comfort zone and do something that scares you because it's one of the most valuable ways in which you can grow as a person and achieve your higher purpose.

Sarah Avis, author of Cancer... The Ultimate Curveball

You never know how strong you are until being strong is the only choice you have. So be strong, stay resilient and when life gives you a thousand reasons to cry, show life that you have a thousand reasons to smile.

Frida Lobo

Say YES to saying yes! Stretch yourself out of your comfort zone daily; doing so will bring many new exciting opportunities into your life.

Linda Berlot

What can you do today to utterly amaze yourself?

GORILLIAS IN RWANDA

I met Nicci Roscoe in 2015 at the NSA (National Speakers Association) conference in Washington. We stayed in touch after the conference and when I asked her for a few words of inspiration for the book she utterly amazed me. Here's her story.

Two years after surviving a brain tumour I was determined to do one thing on my bucket list. I was in constant pain and had swelling in my head. This was a challenge. I refused to allow the pain to prevent me from achieving life's possibilities. There are three titanium plates in my head along with six screws, one of which is loose!

I needed to do something dramatic to show that I was in charge of the pain and that it was not in charge of me. I wanted to climb in the spectacular Virunga Mountains in Rwanda to see their famous gorillas.

Dianne Fossey was my inspiration. She had saved the gorillas from extinction by having the courage to stand up for what she believed. Finding courage to get my life back on track was what I needed and the Virunga Mountains was the place to do it!

As we ascended the mountain the air became thin. This added to the pain in my head. I wouldn't give in to it. After six hours we reached the top. But life isn't always straightforward. We received unwelcome news. The gorillas had gone to the bottom of the mountains! I was exhausted yet still determined to see them.

The descent was more challenging yet there was a moment when I held my breath with total excitement. It was when the most magnificent silverback gorilla suddenly appeared on the trail. He came charging at us. The guide pushed me to the ground for my protection. The gorilla whooshed past then he disappeared!

I was exhilarated. My heart was beating faster than ever before! I'd glimpsed something which, in the worst moments before the tumour operation, I feared I would never see. Life suddenly felt extraordinarily special.

Taking action to climb the mountain despite the pain built my courage and confidence. You can do the same – anything is possible when you really want it.

Nicci Roscoe, International Speaker and author of Fabulous Impact

JUMP FOR A CAUSE

In 2007 we created the Tickled Pink Series – a series of events, master classes and challenges to raise awareness and funds for Brest Friends, a breast cancer support group in Dubai. One of the challenges was to do a tandem skydive in pink jumpsuits. For many people, jumping 12,000 feet out of a perfectly good plane strapped to a man is nothing short of madness and definitely out of many people's comfort zone. We attracted over 50 people to jump for the cause. Many of the people that jumped said that this was way out of their comfort zone, yet they faced their fears and jumped. It was amazing to see how quickly facial expressions, body language and confidence levels can change. During the briefing and the 20-minute flight to jump altitude there were a lot of seriously concerned looking faces and rather strained smiles! Within minutes this changed to 'G Force' smiles for the video camera, a feeling of total freedom… and finally hugs, smiles and squeals of delight after landing in the drop zone. It's the best thing you can do with a man with all your clothes on!

*"Only those who risk going too far will
ever know how far they can go."*
– T. S. Eliot

ALISON'S LEAP OF FAITH

I met Alison in Hong Kong, she was the driving force and the face of Women in Charge, a networking group for professional women business owners in Hong Kong. We often got together to brainstorm ideas for events. One of our ideas was to arrange a jump off Macau Tower on International Women's Day. I could sense Alison was a little wary of setting this up as an event with me as it would mean she had to lead by example and take the leap of faith herself…

'They' say the magic happens when you get out of your comfort zone and if it scares you, it might be a good idea to try! I'll never forget how petrified I was standing at the edge of a drop so insanely high, and the confidence that reverberated throughout my body after that initial step into space! I've done the jump again since, and the overwhelming feeling of accomplishing something you initially thought there was no way in hell you could do is so gratifying that words can't describe it. I've realised that fear is not real, it's a choice – if you run to it, it will run away.

A year later, on International Women's Day 2012, I was in Cambodia embarking on a gruelling 11-day 550km cycling challenge through the breathtaking country to raise funds to help put an end to sexual slavery for the Somaly Mam Foundation – another giant leap of faith! Not a cyclist, I bought a bike and trained for two months prior to jumping on a plane to Phnom Penh and raised over US$10,000 for the innocent victims caught up in the ugly world of human trafficking, some as young as three and sold for just US$50.

A few months later, I took what I'm hoping was my last leap of faith when I left the comfort of a 14-year relationship. It was one of the most difficult things I've ever done but I listened to nobody other than myself and made the tough decision to walk away.

To succeed at any challenge in life, you've got to tune out the noise around you – the footsteps of others, the distracting 'advice' and the doubters who will tell you it can't be done. Instead, focus on your inner voice. Setting your own goal, charting your own course and trusting your own instincts takes courage, yet they are the surest route to crossing your personal finish line. Do what you need to do and do it for you, not for others.

Have faith in you, whether you leap or not! Nobody is going to look after you more than you, so make you a priority, and always be happy. It's free!

Alison Price

CANCEL YOUR SUBSCRIPTION TO THE COMFORT CLUB

JOIN THE I'M ALIVE AND KICKING CLUB

By getting out of your comfort zone more regularly, you will gradually increase the number of things you are comfortable with. You will also be able to enjoy more things in life; the more you do that activity, the more you will enjoy it, and sooner or later it will become second nature. Sign up for the course you've always wanted to do, join a networking group, wear a red dress, travel to a new country, try something new off the menu, say what you really want to say and ask for what you want – these are all simple ways to step out of your comfort zone. It would have been very easy and comfortable for me to stay in a full-time job running a sports facility, instead I chose the path of self-employment and have been able to meet some amazing people, work on incredible projects and travel to so many new countries. Get comfortable being uncomfortable and join the *I'm alive and kicking club*, there are so many amazing opportunities out there just waiting for you.

ANN SADDLES UP FOR THE GOBI CHALLENGE

I met Ann Holliday in Dubai – with a name like Holliday it's no surprise that she loves travelling. In 2013 I put a call out for women warriors to go on the *Jewels of Mongolia* horseback challenge.

The advert read: 'Looking for women warriors to go on a Jewels of Mongolia adventure – must be able to ride a horse.'

As soon as I saw this, I knew I wanted to do this challenge, but there was only one small problem: I had never ridden a horse! I was living in the UK so was fortunate enough to be near several places where I could learn to ride. I had eight weeks to go before the trip so signed up for 12 lessons.

Riding didn't come naturally to me I have to admit, but by the time I had to be on my way to Mongolia, I had picked up the basic principles of how to handle horses, and was able to ride around the paddock at the riding school – not exactly full preparation for the Mongolian Steppes, but it would have to do!

July came around and I was in Mongolia with the team in Terelj National Park staying in a Ger camp. The horses were a lot smaller than those I'd practised on in the UK, and they had local saddles, so it was all quite a bit different from what I'd learnt to ride on. To begin with it was quite scary, but as I got used to the horse, I found that he started to respond (thankfully!) to some of the things that I had learnt in my lessons back in the UK. I quickly realised people ride very differently in Mongolia, and that I'd need to just get used to these differences, and get on with it.

After a few days riding I was feeling more confident about riding and able to relax and enjoy the experience. I still wasn't quite convinced that riding was 'my thing' or if I would do it again, but I did form a great impression of Mongolia and the beauty of its scenery.

My surprise can be imagined then, when a few weeks after returning to UK, my husband found out by bizarre coincidence that his next assignment would be in – wait for it – Mongolia! As my impressions of Mongolia were favourable, I was excited to find that we were soon on our way back out there again. This time for several years!

Some months passed and I got to know about Ulaanbaatar (UB) and the country generally, and was lucky enough to get in with a great group of girlfriends, who eventually asked if I would like to go riding with them. I confessed that I was a bit of a beginner as far as horses were concerned, but said that I'd like to come. A few days later we headed to Saraa's Ger Camp, and when we got there I was thankfully given a horse that was 'easy to manage'. This really helped my confidence, and I continued to ride every week when I was in Mongolia.

My riding improved with each trip, and I started to really look forward to when I could be out in the countryside riding with my new friends. Over lunch one day, one of the girls mentioned that she was organising the next 'Gobi Gallop' – a 10-day horse ride over 700km through the rugged terrain of Mongolia.

It sounded like a once-in-a-lifetime challenge (for me anyway) and so when we went riding the following week, I asked a few more questions about the ride. I didn't ask the most important question out loud, but to myself: Am I riding well enough to do this? My answer back to myself was: I think so – but what condition will you be in after 10 days riding?! There was only one way to find out, and so in 2014, I decided to do the Gobi Gallop and see how I would survive after 700km and 10 days, across one of the remotest places in the world: The Gobi Desert and the Steppes of Outer Mongolia.

It turned out to be one of the most amazing adventures I have ever had. To ride in Outer Mongolia, with not a fence in sight, the occasional Ger, truly breathtaking views, and herds of wild animals roaming and grazing in complete freedom, is really a privilege. I have been on a few adventures in various places in the world, but this for me was one of the most challenging I have ever done. It challenged everything: my body, my mind and my soul. I finished the ride exhausted, but exhilarated – I had not only been able to play a part in raising money for the children of the peak, but I tested my own inner strengths, and was really pleased that I found myself up to the challenge.

Ann Holliday

GET MOVING!

"Whatever you can do or dream you can do, begin it. Boldness has genius, magic and power in it. Begin it now."
– Goethe

The only way to blast through fear is to do the thing you fear; as the NIKE slogan goes: Just do it. Whatever you resist will persist and take a lot of your mental and physical energy in the process. The longer you avoid your fears, the bigger they grow in your mind.

Remember the first time you try something new it's going to feel a little strange, this is very normal. The good thing is that every time you do what you fear, the fear dissolves a little more each time, your confidence grows and before you know it you are feeling totally in charge and even able to smile in the process! Everything you ever wanted is on the other side of fear so face your fears head on. The minute you do, they lose all their power over you.

Fear has lots of different voices: doubt, self-depreciation and criticism to name a few. When you start to name your fears and recognise that's just what they are – fears as opposed to reality – you can start to concentrate more on what action you need to take.

"Life shrinks or expands in proportion to one's courage."
– Anais Nin

WHAT ARE YOU AFRAID OF?

Here are some common fears – highlight or note down the ones which you feel apply to you:

- Fear of rejection

- Fear of failure

- Fear of losing

- Fear of succeeding

- Fear of not being good enough

- Fear of the unknown

- Fear of the future

- Fear of being wrong

- Fear of making a mistake

- Fear of being laughed at

- Fear of not having enough money

- Fear of ??????

I had a fear of not being good enough academically which didn't really make sense as I won a scholarship to attend a private school and went on to university. Writing a book brings out all kinds of fears around being good enough. The only way to get around this fear is to write and be brave enough to share your work, accepting that it might not be everyone's cup of tea and that's totally OK. Damned if you do, damned if you don't. Finishing this book was nothing short of a miracle and indicates that I have almost let the fear of not being good enough go.

I have learnt that one of the simplest ways to ease fears is to acknowledge them rather than try to escape them. While you run from your fears they will keep chasing you so stand still look at them, and ask yourself where the fear is coming from. What exactly are you afraid of and why – write down your answers until you get to the source. Is it based on a previous experience, did you try something once and it didn't work so you are afraid to try it again? Instead of remaining fearful, be ready to learn, to change and find someone to help you overcome your fears. If you are afraid of speaking in public, sign up for a course in public speaking. For the most part fears are false evidence appearing real rather than reality. Act on them rather than letting them act on you. As Susan Jeffers says, "Feel the fear and do it anyway".

Fear is useful, it helps protect you from potential harm; it's also a sign that something exciting is about to happen so use it to take opportunities even when your knees are knocking! Whatever you do, don't let fear keep you from your destiny. It helps to want something more than you are afraid of it. The power of wanting it more than the feeling of fearing it will compel you to make the first move.

$25,000 BACK-UP AND AIKIDO COURAGE

Taking action is not always about jumping out of planes, climbing mountains or riding wild horses in Mongolia. For many it could be moving country or speaking in front of an audience. For Ginny, it was leaving a great career to write a book and start the Institute of Zen Leadership.

When I was working at NASA, it was becoming increasingly clear to me that my career needed to shift. For several years, the contrast between what I was seeing at NASA and in the dojo had been gnawing on me. At work I was watching people get more stressed out, worn down and defensive. On the mat, I was seeing people develop greater resilience, energy and courage. NASA had enrolled me in a series of Leadership Development programs to prepare me for the government's Senior Executive Service, but instead these programs were showing me how much I wanted to be teaching them, bringing in Zen, Aikido, and body-mind as one.

NASA had other plans for me. And for a while, I was able to ride both rails, continuing to work for NASA while I took steps in a new direction. I started writing a book about learning through the body, building a practice of writing daily. I had to support myself, so I looked at my finances and settled on a number – $25,000 – that I had to save up before I would be willing to leap from the security of steady income. I figured I could live on that for six months and, in that time, could figure out something – even if it meant going back to waiting tables (which I did through college). But what really gave me courage was Aikido. Because Aikido is a throwing art, I'd had years of practice taking falls. And something in me KNEW it could take a fall and get up again. That physical knowing gave me courage.

So all of these things helped me make the leap from NASA with only two days of work lined up for the rest of my life. In so doing, I turned down another promotion at NASA, which completely angered one of my favourite leaders at the Johnson Space Center who had been a dear mentor. She never spoke to me again. And my father was so mad at me, he thought I'd lost my mind. Yet somehow that day, I got my life back. Up to that point, I had done everything *expected of me. After that point, I did the work that was mine to do. And I never did have to touch the $25,000, nor wait tables.*

Dr Ginny Whitelaw, author of The Zen Leader

NO SUCH THING AS FAILURE – ONLY FEEDBACK

There is no such thing as failure, only feedback. The goal is to take action on the feedback until you succeed in what you are aiming to achieve. I invite you to say yes to opportunities that will stretch and grow you, and if at first you don't succeed, try, try again. Not achieving the outcome that you desire usually means it's time to step back, look at what needs to change, what you can do differently and then give it another go. I have done this a few times in my life…

In August 2013 Calin and I signed up to climb Mount Elbrus, the highest peak in Europe and one of the seven continental summits standing at 5642m. We had put plenty of training in and looked forward to meeting the team and going for the summit. Having previously reached a personal best of 7000m on a peak in Tibet we were confident we would be good to go.

On summit night we left camp with the group and our guides at 2am. Elbrus is not technically challenging yet still requires advanced snow and ice climbing skills. One of the main challenges is the very changeable weather, in particular strong winds.

About one hour into the climb the mild weather we had been enjoying for the past few days changed into 55mph winds and constant snowfall making it difficult to cut and keep a path. With the conditions the way they were it was not possible to take regular breaks for water or food as we had been doing over the previous days. We just had to keep going, head down and bracing ourselves against the wind. Just 342m away from the summit one of the guides who had been ahead of our group came to us and explained the conditions higher up were not safe and advised us to turn around and head back to base camp. Calin and I looked at each other through our snow and ice ridden goggles, at the time we were both pretty exhausted. We were disappointed that we were so close to the summit and were not able to continue; however, we always put our own life and safety first and it was clear the mountain gods had other plans for us that day, it was time to turn around and head back to base camp. Calin is a big guy at 1.88m and weighing in at 110kg. I'm 1.63m and weighed in at 65kg on this climb so I had been blown about like a tiny Russian doll all the way up and down the mountain.

Back at base camp I kept repeating in my mind there is no such thing as failure only feedback and that the mountain would still be here next year. I was really running on empty and had nothing left to give to the mountain, this was tough for me to accept and made me question so many things about myself. Did I train hard enough, what could I do better to prepare for heavy winds, what had happened to my energy levels, had I been doing too much before the climb? Where was the self-doubt and tears coming from? Yes, I have my moments of vulnerability too!

HAVE THE COURAGE TO START AND BE WILLING TO KEEP AT IT TILL YOU REACH YOUR GOAL

350 days later, after our first attempt on Elbrus, Calin and I went back to Russia, hired a private guide and gave it a second shot. This time coming back home without summiting was not an option. We would stay until we had made it all the way to the top and had planned in extra days on the mountain to take into account the variable weather conditions. We had both put in extra training and had summited on Kilimanjaro a few days before we left for Russia

so were already well acclimatised. The weather was a little kinder, we had reprogrammed our minds for summit success, our guide was great and we had rested and eaten well. As we were only two we could make decisions with the guide on when to push for the summit based on the weather forecast so could act quickly and take advantage of any clear weather windows. We did and made it to the top! Instead of tears of disappointment there were tears of joy at the summit. Finishing off that last 342 metres and reaching the top meant so much to both of us; besides, if I can't walk my talk and practise what I preach, how can I expect to inspire others to stick to their goals until they are reached?

ONE FOOT IN FRONT OF THE OTHER

The quickest way to build courage and confidence is to keep trying new things – and doing more of them. My dear friend Ros is living proof that taking action leads to a very fulfilling and adventurous life.

Since childhood, I've had a fascination with heights. I was lucky enough to grow up among the mountains of Cyprus, delighting in scrambling to the top of a rock and claiming it as 'mine'. Later, in Iran, the UAE and Oman, where my career took me, I would seek new and more daring ways up the jebels (Arabic word for mountains) with like-minded friends. Inevitably, I suppose, I hankered after 'real' climbing and enrolled myself in climbing school in Switzerland, thence moving on to high-altitude mountaineering across the continents, where I relished the challenge and conversely the simplicity of the focus on a single goal.

While living in Sharjah, UAE, one of the world's flatter spots, I noticed an advertisement for a trek to Everest Base Camp and thought I'd respond, hoping to meet other mountain-minded people. I duly set off for Kathmandu with a remarkable multinational team of women; Julie, the inspiration behind the trip, was my tent-mate and we would happily fantasise together about possible future adventures.

The next year saw me in Jordan with Julie and a similar team, this time on an expedition which included mountain biking, horse and camel riding, rock scrambling, canyoning with a dramatic abseil through a waterfall, and tandem skydiving. After the considerable apprehension of taking off in a tiny Cessna, strapped to an instructor in an unfamiliar harness and knowing we had to jump out at 10,000 feet, came the magic of floating down into Wadi Rum at sunset amid the spectacular rose and earthen colours of the rock walls surrounding us.

My next adventure with Julie was a climb of Kilimanjaro by the Machame route. Arduous but satisfying daily treks through ever-changing vegetation zones were followed by evenings in the mess tent swapping stories with a lively and diverse group of team mates. The air grew thinner and the trails steeper, but finally, after a seemingly interminable summit night, we stood on Uhuru Peak in the early morning surrounded by misty mountain ranges stretching far into the distance. It was a good place to be.

Expeditions are more than a hobby; they're a way of life which keeps calling one back. For those who ask how one does it: you just have to decide to go and then put one foot in front of the other.

As Thoreau said, "Go confidently in the direction of your dreams. Live the life you have imagined."

I hope I always will.

Dr Rosalind Buckton-Tucker

THE ABILITY TO TAKE ACTION EVEN WHEN THE OUTCOME IS UNCERTAIN

It's fair to say that confidence is one of the essential ingredients for living a fulfilled life and forms part of your overall well-being, success and happiness. If you have little or no self-confidence it's easy to find yourself feeling and staying stuck. For many people confidence is a feeling they only experience when they can be 100% sure that the outcome will be successful. I tend to lean more towards confidence being the ability to take action even when the outcome is uncertain. If you only take action when you are 100% sure of the outcome, you might 'stay safe' but will miss out on so many opportunities. Besides, can you ever be totally certain about an outcome? If you don't believe you can do something and have doubts about your ability to do it, there is a tendency to take less action or none at all. Whatever you believe will be true for you, it becomes a self-fulfilling prophecy.

"Aerodynamically the bumblebee should not be able to fly…
but the bumblebee doesn't know that,
so it goes on flying anyway."

– Mary Kay Ash

 **BRIGHT IDEA:**

From now onwards, how about taking one risk per week, or per day if you like! Trying out new experiences will take you out of your comfort zone, lessen your fear of the unknown and boost your confidence. It doesn't have to be extreme – it could be something as simple as wearing a red dress instead of the usual black one you wear, attending a networking event and talking to people you don't know instead of staying with the ones you do.

KNOW THYSELF

Questions are the answer so have a think about the answers to the questions below and take a few minutes to jot them down in your journal. Remember, awareness precedes change.

1. What do you tend to avoid due to a lack of confidence?

2. What would you do if you had more confidence?

3. Who are your role models of confidence – what is it about them that makes them confident?

4. What's the scariest thing you have ever done?

5. What do you do currently with total confidence and how can you transfer this level of confidence to other areas of your life?

 **BRIGHT IDEA:**

Start a confidence log within your journal and list down the things you have achieved in all areas of your life to date (career, finance, relationships etc.). See how successful and confident you are already! Note down the things you would like to start doing with more confidence and who can help you get started – what's your first action step?

FISH OUT OF WATER

Confidence is environment, relationship and context specific. You might feel totally confident in one environment yet feel like a fish out of water in others. You might be fine in a one-to-one situation yet freeze when you are at a networking event. Here are a few seemingly universal situations in which people would like to be more confident:

- Learning a new skill

- Speaking in public

- Networking

- Starting or ending a relationship

- Changing careers

- Moving country

- Being a parent

- Asking for a pay rise

- Writing a book!

I am sure you can add others to the list above. Remember, awareness precedes change. Revisit the A.U.D.R.E.Y. principle from Chapter 2 and start shifting from awareness to your Eureka YES! moment with TOTAL CONFIDENCE knowing that taking action, however small it is, builds your courage and confidence muscles!

REMEMBER TO CELEBRATE

Mastering new things gives you the confidence to try other new things. Success breeds success. When you are willing to step out of your comfort zone you can do it again, and again… and again. You will find that you start to actually do more things instead of just thinking about them. Confidence and courage make great partners in action, think of them as muscles that need working out every day. Remember to celebrate your success however small or large you feel it. Give yourself a pat on the back, have a massage, treat yourself and those you love to something special to mark your achievement, it will give you an additional boost to keep achieving more.

A FEW WORDS ON WORDS

When you change 'I can't' to 'I can' you shift your energy into what's possible. To help you speak with more confidence here are a few words I suggest you eliminate from your vocabulary:

TRY – change to I WILL

HOPE – change to I AM MAKING PLANS TO…

BUT – change to AND or HOWEVER

SHOULD – change to I HAVE CHOSEN or DECIDED to…

WISH – change to I AM COMMITTED to…

CAN'T – I CAN

Tap into the power of your words, it's amazing how different you will feel.

And now for something completely different…

POWER ANIMALS

I first connected with the concept of power animals after reading the book by Gary Leboff titled *DARE – Take Your Life on and Win*. One of the exercises in the book was to create a film in your mind and think of a time when you felt truly alive, confident and wonderful. What were you doing? Where were you? How did you feel? During the film you had to imagine what kind of animal you felt you most resembled. I did the exercise and saw myself standing on top of a mountain; my power animal was a lion standing proud and strong at the summit with the wind blowing through its mane as it looked out to a whole new world. Just a few days after doing this exercise I saw a fabulous oil canvas painting of a lion's head with a gorgeous mane in a local art shop; I bought it and to this day keep it in my office on the wall looking over my desk. Any time

I need to power up I stand in the 'rocky pose', imagine myself on the summit of a mountain and look straight into the lion's eyes and ask for insights; I literally imagine what the lion would like me to know to move forward courageously. You might think this is 'Fu Fu' and that's OK!

Be open to everything – it works for me!

BRIGHT IDEA:

Stop reading now and give the power animal exercise a go. Think of a time when you were feeling totally confident, courageous and unstoppable; if you were to be an animal, what animal would you be? Write down the answer in your journal or make a note of it here in the book then research all the characteristics of your animal and see how they relate to you. How can you bring more of these traits into other areas of your life?

MOUNTAIN LION – BEARS – KOKOPELLIS

In 2007 my mother-in-law, Alice, gave me a Zuni bear necklace fetish with a Kokopelli carved into it for Christmas; that same Christmas I was given a book on Native American wisdom and some slate coasters with Hopi and Zuni characters on them. These gifts further ignited my interest in power animals and their specific meanings. Years later I find myself writing this chapter on a road trip to Sedona where every other shop is full of crystals and power animals with specific qualities – qualities to include action, courage and confidence! An intuitive reading I had a few months back reveals that my spirit animal is a mountain lion – no surprises there! Hours later I am the proud owner of a honey onyx mountain lion fetish found in a fabulous shop called Garlands along Oak Creek Canyon, Sedona – you have to go there when you next visit Sedona!

In the shamanic belief everything is alive and carries with it power and wisdom. Shamans believe that everyone has power animals/ animal spirits that reside in each individual adding to their personal power. Not everyone relates to power animals, maybe you relate more to guardian angels, talismans, symbols, mantras, all of which you can tap into when you need a boost of courage. You can actually use anything that 'speaks' to you or something that you have a strong emotional attachment to; maybe it's something that represents a milestone or a special person in your life. I have a small pewter Viking warrior that Jannike gave me from Norway, a sea glass angel from Cape Cod that Ginny gave me on the Camino, a penguin pendant from Susanne, a Wandela bracelet from Val, several special crystals and rocks from around the globe and a small Quan Yin (a bodhisattva associated with compassion) I picked up in Hong Kong. They don't all come with me on my travels – I usually pick one to go! Maybe it's a piece of jewellery or something else that you wear or a small picture of someone or something you love – whatever works for you!

It's time to switch off again, you know what to do!

1. **MEDITATE**

2. **COME TO YOUR SENSES**

3. **AFFIRMATION**
   I am Committed to Taking Action

4. **POWER OF THREE**

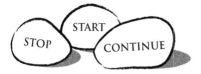

What are you going to start, stop and continue doing as a result of reading this chapter?

What's your 'TAKING ACTION BUILDS COURAGE AND CONFIDENCE' STORY?

Write it now.

What are you excited, committed and grateful for in relation to this chapter? Jot your thoughts down in your journal or on the Notes pages at the end of the book – and then move on to the next chapter!

FOLLOW
YOUR CALLING

CHAPTER 5

EXPLORE AND DISCOVER YOUR PLACE IN THE WORLD

"Life is an adventure – live it! Explore and discover the freedom to be who you truly are, the courage and confidence to believe in your wildest dreams, the wisdom to follow your heart and discover your place in the world.

The world is round – go around it."

– Julie Miles Lewis

GIFT OF THE GLOBE

When I was seven years old my father bought me a globe. We used to sit together and spin it then I would close my eyes and stop it spinning with my finger. Wherever my finger landed we would have a lively discussion about what was special about that country, what language people spoke, what kind of terrain was most prominent – mountains, forests, icebergs, snow; what beliefs, traditions and culture existed, the type of clothes they wore. I learnt so much more through these fun discussions than I ever did in geography classes at school!

Whenever we played the spinning globe game my mind went into overdrive and more often than not I would have wild dreams about the country we had discussed; in my dreams I saw myself mushing through the snow with a team of huskies, being on safari in Africa, climbing mountains in Nepal.

The next day in school I would tell my classmates about my adventures and invite them to join me at break time in the school yard where we would play make believe and get lost in a whole new world. Little did I know at that time that 34 years later I would be leading expeditions to many of the places we talked about. I had no idea about bucket lists at the age of 7, I know now and also believe whether you are 7 or 70 it's never too early or too late to write your list, start living your wildest dreams and find your place or places in the world.

If you haven't already got a globe or a large map I highly recommend investing in them for your home and your office. It's an easy way to give all those who set their eyes on it a more global perspective and it's a great gift to give to your children.

YOUR PLACE IN THE WORLD

Wherever you are in the world right now having a map or a globe makes it easy to pinpoint your geographical place in the world and see all the other places you would like to visit and maybe even move to. Venturing and exploring new places is easier than ever; the world is so much smaller than it was for our parents and grandparents. We can be pretty much anywhere, anytime. Ready, steady, pack and go. Planes, trains, cars... and galactic adventures on the horizon!

If you can't get out into the world, digital technology brings the world to you. More than ever we can stay connected even when we are geographically miles apart. Skype has opened up a whole new world. You can share your world with family and friends anywhere around the globe real time. Within seconds you can post pictures on social media allowing hundreds, maybe thousands of people to be on a virtual journey with you. Now more than ever it's possible to explore and discover your place in the world and keep track of where everyone else is in relation to your world.

 **BRIGHT IDEA:**
Get a wall map and mount it on a cork board, put pins in all the places you have been to in one colour, all the places you would like to go to in another colour, and all the places you have friends or family in another colour – you will be amazed how much of the earth you are actually part of in some way. Pin it and post on Pinterest! The world is round so go around it!

MOMENTS OF CLARITY IN A BHUTANESE MONASTERY

Sometimes clarity of your place in the world comes in the wildest of places...

Holidays for most people are a time for forgetting everything and just having fun. But they can also prove to be the catalyst for life-changing events. In 2008, I found myself enrolling on a boot camp fitness course in preparation for one of Mountain High's challenges. I had let my fitness levels slip in the first two years of living in Dubai. The Cyprus activity challenge was nine months away and I wanted to be in the best shape possible. My fitness level soon came back to its highest in many a year and I was revelling in the exercise environment, gently encouraging and motivating those in my group with lower fitness levels than myself.

The Cyprus challenge came and went, along with other Mountain High trips to Peru, Vietnam and Cape Town in subsequent years. It was whilst walking the Inca Trail during the Peruvian trip that my mind became open to a total change in career. I was an office manager for a leading international law firm, having been in the office environment for almost 25 years at that point. I wanted to strive for increased fitness levels for myself and I wanted to give people the fitness tools to be able to undertake walks like that, to live as independent and healthy a life as possible for as long as they could.

I enrolled on a Personal Fitness Instructor course, which I passed in 2012, and a subsequent specialist qualification in training over 40s. My plan was for the change of career on leaving Dubai a few years down the line. During a holiday to Bhutan in 2013, inside an almost derelict monastery perched on top of a hill, I had a moment of clarity. It was sudden and it took me by total surprise. I remember walking outside and tying up my prayer flags with the help of the monks, looking across the stunning landscape, deciding that the day I returned to the office I was going to resign – and that's what I did. The first day back in the office after the trip was my 25th anniversary at the law firm.

I am now just over a year into my new life as a personal trainer, loving every waking moment, even if most mornings that wake-up call is at 5am. The reward of receiving feedback from clients that their rheumatoid *arthritis or herniated discs symptoms have eased, or that they have a waist for the first time in 30 years, or that they have more energy now than ever before makes me feel that I have found my vocation. This new life has also granted me one of my lifetime wishes – to have the flexibility to travel more often, to all those places still missing a pin on my world travel map.*

I would never have thought when I met up with Jules for my first Mountain High adventure that my journey would have taken me to where I am today – of finding my true place in the world.

Louise Halmakan, TuVida LLC

FIGURE OUT WHAT YOU REALLY WANT TO DO

Life is frustrating when you are not doing what you were really put on this planet to do. When I came back from my first mountain climb on Kota Kinabalu I started writing out a list of all the things I was curious and passionate about. I noted what my strengths were and asked a few trusted friends and colleagues what they perceived as my strengths. It soon became very clear that the times I felt totally alive and "most on purpose" was when I was in nature, travelling, connecting with new cultures, learning new skills, sharing my passion for the great outdoors with others and encouraging people, in particular women, to realise their own ambitions. It was a no brainer to change my role as business development manager and start Mountain High.

Sometimes even when you have a great job and are enjoying the lifestyle it brings with it you still might feel there is something more you want to be doing; the challenge is to find out what! Sometimes you can't see it for yourself, it takes someone else to give you a nudge. I met Mike at a business seminar in Dubai. I am sure his story will resonate with some of you.

For around 49 years I thought I knew my place in the world as that's where I had ended up. I was a successful international corporate general manager living in one of the most exciting cities where I had and still have the privilege of watching it grow from a child into its teenage years and now entering adulthood.

It seemed I had it all: a well-paid job with all the trimmings (including the obligatory Jag!), a very happy and fulfilling personal life with my soul mate and wife Claire and our small but growing family of rescue cats.

However, there had been something inside of me trying to get out and make itself known to me for some time and over a period of time around four years ago, it became more of a discomfort as I tried to figure out what it was and what I was supposed to do about it. The best way of describing this feeling is that it was like a calling out to me that there was still a lot for me to achieve and retirement at the age of 50 (which had always been what I thought a good goal to be) was not an option. In fact it would be irresponsible as I was being told that there were a lot more people out there that needed my help by me doing what I do best: growing people and businesses. But I would need a physical push for me to give up all the trimmings I had worked so hard for over 27 years in corporate life.

After long discussions at home and with other close friends and colleagues, one morning I woke with the usual 6.00am alarm call and to Claire saying to me, "You know Mike, the problem is that you just haven't done what you really want to do, so go out there and help people grow themselves and their businesses, you owe it to them." So I did just that and now have the privilege of working with some of the brightest and most enthusiastic SME business owners here in Dubai as I get them moving and guide them on their own scaling–up journey. I now feel I have found my true place in the world.

Mike, Mike Hoff Consulting

YOUR PLACE IN THE WORLD

Where do you feel most at home in the world? Where do you find yourself living a connected full life filled with peace, joy, love and laughter to neutralise and balance all the challenges of 21st century living? Where do you feel most alive? There is no right or wrong answer, it really is whatever feels right for you; it can often change with the seasons, your mood, or during personal and professional transitions. Sometimes you crave to be alone or for connection to others: your partner, family, friends, animals, or to nature. Sometimes you don't really know where you want to be and who you want to be with – that's OK, at least for a while.

Maybe it's in the city, in the mountains, on the ocean, in a forest, on a football pitch, on a stage, on a deserted island, in an igloo, tree house, tent, on a bike – you get the idea! More than likely it's a combination of many places and spaces depending on what your soul is craving for at the time.

"There is nothing like returning to a place that remains unchanged to find the ways in which you yourself have altered."

– Nelson Mandela

If you have lived overseas for a period of time, moving back to your home country can often turn out to be another opportunity to rediscover your place in the world.

Catherine's coming home story…

Having lived and worked in different locations overseas for 15 years, my partner and I made the decision to return home to the UK permanently. I thought settling back into London would be the easiest move of all. How wrong could I be! Clearly, I was not the only one to make this assumption. Friends and family had the expectation that 'coming home is easy' and were surprised to see me struggle initially.

Society had moved on, life in general had changed so much; ways of doing things were different. Being 'home' was strange and unfamiliar and proving to be a nightmare. Yet, I was constantly being asked how I was enjoying being home. On the career front, I soon discovered my professional experience had no direct fit; prospective employers were unsure or simply not interested in my overseas experience. Having left a dynamic and exciting work environment I felt like I'd be catapulted into premature retirement.

Initially, the realisation that full-time employment was not a viable option felt like a disappointing blow but in reality it proved to be a wonderful opportunity. Now was the time to be creative; to do something that I'd always been very interested in and on the fringes of, professionally, for a long time. I decided to train as a psychotherapist. Much of my career has been training, coaching and human development so the opportunity to train in psychotherapy was a dream come true.

On completing the demanding four-year postgraduate training I set up my own small private practice. Grateful for the opportunities I have been given over the course of my life, I also felt it was time to give something back, so I work in an honorary capacity one day a week in a London NHS hospital and also as a voluntary counsellor for a national charity. My life is now busy and dynamic in a very different and rewarding way.

With hindsight and professional insight, I can see that the underlying feeling around my return was a huge sense of loss: loss of my overseas home, my professional identity, my friends, my lifestyle, the things and routines that were familiar to me. Though completely unaware of this initially, once I began to see and acknowledge that, in fact, I was grieving for the things I'd left behind, it helped to make sense of why, in the early stages of being back, I had such intense feelings of sadness, anger and rage. It has also allowed me to accept and move on to appreciate wonderful gains I have had from my 'coming home' experience: an exciting new career, a business, a beautiful new home, being closer to my family, renewed contact with old friends... the list goes on.

What I have learnt from this is the importance of having a vision, as well as the willingness to change course and be flexible as needs and circumstances dictate. If we remain fixed, focusing on just one thing, we may fail to see other opportunities on the horizon.

Catherine Musto, Psychotherapist & Awareness Coach

A LIFE ON THE OCEAN WAVES

I met Wendy through my dear friends Jean and Paul who adopted us both as their surrogate daughters at a time when we needed a base camp (home) before moving on again in the world. Exchanging life on dry land for life on the ocean waves gave Wendy an opportunity to explore many new places in a very different world.

By the ripe old age of 21, taking myself out of my comfort zone had already become a way of life. I had been engaged, become un-engaged and travelled on a one-way ticket to New York with a backpack, my bestie and nowhere to stay. I had trained as a croupier and worked the exciting casino life in a top London club but sadly faced swift redundancy, so when my dream job of working on cruise ships landed in my lap, the answer was a resounding yes! As the train carried me and my lone piece of luggage to my new life, I wondered why this challenge felt so daunting.

For the first time, I had serious misgivings, taking the return journey to London seemed a far more comfortable option, returning to my friends, family and familiarity. Fortunately I persuaded myself that golden opportunities come once in a blue moon and decided to push on to another level in my life, one of exploration, achievement and endless golden memories. Settling for a life of mediocrity was never going to fulfil me, and my leap of faith paid off. I enjoyed the privilege of learning about cultures, people and their respective countries for 10 enriching years, gleaning life experiences from every continent in the world and deeply nourishing my soul.

My profound gratitude to the universe for guiding me onwards and upwards and for giving me the clarity of mind to make the best decision I could for my personal growth. My advice is to be open to seeing an opportunity for what it is, then grab it – with both hands.

Wendy Hulbert, author of My Brother Edward, A Memoir

THE POWER OF PLACES

When I look at pictures of places I feel drawn to, I ask myself: What is it in this picture that I am longing for? Often specific places, sacred mountains, pilgrimage trails, oceans, forests, and other geographical locations are the outer representation of the needs of your inner map. Certain parts of the world have a magnetic pull to them and possess a power to bring about change in ways you could rarely access if you were to remain at home. When I look at mountains I feel peace, when I see forests I think of growth, I want to walk through them and hug trees! When I look at the ocean I want to dive into it. When I see vast open spaces of snow I see purity. When I see a beach I think of relaxing in the sun, wiggling my toes in the sand and of times spent with family. I can even smell the sun tan lotion! Start to notice what feelings spring to your mind when you look at pictures of certain places. Next time you look at a picture of a place you feel drawn to, think about what internal craving it is calling to. Where will you choose to go to experience the feelings and cravings such images elicit in you?

LIVING ON AUTOPILOT

It's easy to live on autopilot, running the same routine day in day out, busy with life. Home – work – school – shopping – restaurant – health club – friends – family – everyday life. Where is the space for just 'being' instead of constantly 'doing'? It's easy to take things or people for granted when you are running on autopilot. Autopilot seems to be the norm for many people. How often do you experience life rather than just go through it? Autopilot allows us to do many tasks in a day without being totally present yet mindfulness asks us to stop multi-tasking and be totally present for the one task in hand before starting the next one. This makes sense to me as I have found that jumping from one thing to another is more time consuming and often leads to errors. Do you take phone calls and eat lunch on the go when you are driving… stop it! On treks I encourage people to take mindful breaks to look around, to see where they have come from, where they are going and take in the scenery instead of racing along the trail with their head down. I also suggest they close their eyes and simply feel the warmth of the sun, the breeze and what they can hear instead of see. Nature is a gift to be experienced, step out of autopilot and into NOW so you can experience it with all your senses and be totally present.

"Twenty years on from now you will be more disappointed by the things you didn't do than by the things you did do. So throw off the bowlines. Sail away from the safe harbor. Catch the trade winds in your sails. Explore, dream, discover."

– Mark Twain

CHANCE MEETINGS IN HONG KONG

Calin and I lived in Hong Kong for a couple of years and met lots of new people who we still stay in touch with. It's amazing how chance meetings can develop into lifelong friendships, adventures and meeting people who love exploring their place in their world. Meet Karin, she's truly one of them.

It all started with a book plucked out of a 'grab bag' barrel: Magellan's Journeys. I was too young to read it and my mother nearly exchanged the tome for a younger girl's toy. I clung vigorously. Exploration is in me. Like my father. Always questioning, searching for clues, answers. I read the Madeline and Curious George books and moved on to anthropology, archaeology, history and Chinese, all the while wondering: Why am I here? Serendipity is my friend. And I, hers. I am asked by younger girls, "How have you come this far?" I answer, "No plan." At this stage, I'm a 'lock and leave' girl, questing inwards and outwards, and gorgeously able to recognise and accept opportunities which I stumble across. Some things are years in the making. Travelling with Jules is one of them. Meeting in Hong Kong for a fleeting moment resulted in galloping horses across the expanse of Mongolia, trekking across an Omani desert to the sea and an expedition to the ends of the earth – Antarctica. I'm just getting started. My place in the world is simply being here, thriving in every moment and being open to the next moment of wonder.

Karin Malmstrom

"When a great adventure is offered, you don't refuse it."

– Amelia Earhart

ANSWERING THE CALL

Following your calling is one of the most important and fulfilling ways to unlock your highest potential and experience more joy in your life; the alternative is boredom and a slow emotional death. Merriam-Webster defines a "calling" as "... a strong inner impulse towards a particular course of action especially when accompanied by conviction of divine influence". What strong desires are calling you to do a certain kind of work, to live or travel to certain places or develop closer relationships with people so very different from you? Big and small callings give you the opportunity to experience more of what brings you alive, a way to bring your love, special talents and energy to the world.

Warning – it's not always easy to follow your callings, they often defy logic or what people around you perceive as being normal. "Get a proper job, why do you want to do that , you should be doing this, how could you give up a great career, it's dangerous, it's silly, how could you leave your hometown, what will your parents / peers / friends think"… any of these sound familiar?

Maybe you even question your calling, challenge your own fears, or agonise over a "should, pros and cons list" in an attempt to please everyone. Be true to yourself, when you are everyone around you reaps the benefits.

Callings often start as gentle whispers and get louder and louder until they have your full attention. Sometimes it's repetitive signs, conversations, clues or messages you get out of the blue that "wake" you up to your calling. On a flight back from Hong Kong to Dubai I watched a movie *Mr Popper's Penguins*, I was then served a coffee and a biscuit that just happened to be a Penguin biscuit. A few days later on my 50th birthday I was given a book *Things to Do Now You are Fifty* the page I first opened read "Go to Antarctica". I put out the call for a team of women and within months had recruited the first and only team of breast cancer survivors to go to Antarctica, a videographer and sponsors to get team kit, produce a film and a book – amazing what happens when you follow your calling!

I can recall numerous callings and trust I will answer many more before I leave planet Earth. At 18 I was called to study sports science; I was called to leave Yorkshire to work in Kuwait at 27 when all my friends were getting married and having kids; called to escape from Kuwait during the Gulf crisis; called to climb a mountain three years after being widowed; called to start Mountain High; called to raise awareness for women's health; called to race in a snake boat in Kerala; study Zen; and now called to write a book and develop a speaking career!

I get lots of calls to travel to wild places, I have a hunch that this will be a lifelong calling, as will be my calling to enable others to realise and act on their own callings.

Being true to your calling takes courage and trust. I encourage you to trust the process and believe that everything will unfold at exactly the right time for you. If it doesn't it wasn't right for you and something or someone better will soon call. At some point you will realise that the redundancy, divorce, new job offer, death or birth of a loved one were all life lessons on the path to your true calling. Mentors, guides, money and resources show up out of nowhere; everything flows, some people will think you are crazy, others will be relieved to see you in your "element" and have finally found your place in the world.

Who and where you are now has been shaped by you answering or not answering your calling. Are you feeling fulfilled or empty? If you are feeling empty, off purpose, bored, low on energy or stuck in a unhealthy situation or relationship you may well find yourself taking comfort in food, drink, the TV, retail therapy – anything to mask the pain of not being who you were born to be and doing what you were born to do. What are you hungry, thirsty or yearning for right now? What special gifts reside within you that need to be shared with the world… stop being selfish and share them!

It's up to you to decide, discover, develop and dedicate yourself to your calling, just as it is up to you to not answer certain calls – you know, the ones that take you away from your true calling like the job or the partner everyone thinks was made for you yet feels so incredibly wrong to you – let them go.

Resist the temptation to ignore your calls, they will keep ringing louder and louder until you answer them – or choose to cut the line! Sometimes it takes years to answer the call, sometimes we decide that the call is meant for someone else and pass it up. You will intuitively know when it's time to answer the call – the question is will you? "Follow the Yellow Brick Road", "beam me up Scottie" and "may the Force be with you!"

"And then the day came when the risk to remain tight in a bud was more painful than the risk it took to blossom"

– Anais Nin

 ## BRIGHT IDEA:

Bright Idea: Stop reading for a moment and have some fun with this exercise. Complete the statement: I know it's time to answer the call when…

Answers in your journal please. Make a list of what is calling you however wild it may seem. When you have identified the time to answer the call and what your calling is, think about what's actually stopping you. Write down your list of reasons (excuses) for not making the move. What will happen if you don't make the move? What will happen if you do make the move?

QUESTIONS TO HELP YOU ANSWER YOUR CALLING

When you are giving thought to your calling it might help you to ask the following questions on a regular basis until there is no other option than to take the call. Pick up your journal and start answering the questions below:

1. Who am I? (big question I know)

2. What am I on this planet for?

3. What's my message to the world?

4. What do I stand for?

5. What are my key strengths/natural gifts?

6. What brings me joy and what am I curious about?

7. How am I different?

8. How can I make a difference?

If this is too much all at once just start with one question and write any and all answers that pop into your head and keep writing until you have an answer that makes you cry – more often than not this is your true calling.

> *"Move and the way will open."*
>
> – Zen proverb

Time to follow the same routine as in previous chapters.

1. **MEDITATE**

2. **COME TO YOUR SENSES**

3. **AFFIRMATION**
    I have the World in my Hands

4. **POWER OF THREE**

What are you going to start, stop and continue doing as a result of reading this chapter?

What's your 'EXPLORE AND DISCOVER YOUR PLACE IN THE WORLD' STORY?

Write it now.

What are you excited, committed and grateful about in relation to this chapter? Jot your thoughts down in your journal or on the Notes pages at the end of the book – and then move on to the next chapter!

I AM ANOTHER YOU

CHAPTER 6

YOU HAVE TO CHANGE WHERE YOU ARE TO SEE THINGS DIFFERENTLY

"Change the way you look at things and the things you look at change."

– Wayne W. Dyer

CHANGE IS AN INSIDE JOB

Change is an inside job; when you change your inner thoughts, feelings, emotions and beliefs your outside world changes. Some would argue that it doesn't actually matter where you are geographically. If your inner world is chaotic and your focus is on everything that is not right, this is what tends to show up in your life. That said, there is nothing like hiking up a mountain for you to see things differently! Where and what can you go and do to change your perspective?

VIEW FROM THE SUMMIT

The Chinese have an expression 'shang shan' (to go uphill) to escape the pressure of daily life and see things from a different perspective. It's not always easy to head up a hill or hike up a mountain, although I highly recommend you do!

I must say climbing my first mountain gave me a whole new perspective on life, and a whole new career. It's fair to say that I was a different person at the summit from the person I was at base camp. The belief in my potential heightened with every step I took. The differing views from base camp, along the trail, and finally on the summit offered many new insights along the way. On the way up I took time to stop and look behind me to see where I had been and just how far I had already come. From the summit I could see the journey I had taken and the kind of terrain crossed (most of the summit push is in the dark wearing a headlamp so you only see a few metres ahead of you!). It became clear to me that it was not the actual standing on the summit that had changed me, it was the journey I had experienced getting there. High up in the clouds at 4095m I could see a very different view from where I started. I saw a whole new world waiting to be explored and a whole new chapter of my life unravelling.

GAINING PERSPECTIVE

I have journeyed with many people who also relate to seeing things differently from a summit of a mountain. There is definitely something about being in nature and gaining altitude to awaken, heal and inspire you. It might not be everyone's way of moving on yet I am sure you will feel inspired to access your inner mountain and maybe even climb one after reading Val's story.

I have always loved mountains and am fascinated by the adventurers who climb them. My interest is in the power of the human spirit and what people have to overcome to achieve their goals. Endurance, risk taking, bravery, physical strength, perseverance, focus, vision, a sense of purpose, a natural curiosity for exploration, a love of nature and most of all – NO FEAR.

Hiking is one of my great passions. I have been fortunate and so grateful to hike some memorable trails like the Drakensberg Mountains in South Africa, a volcanic island in Antarctica, Everest Base Camp, Mount Fiji and a few other volcanic calderas around the world. 'See mountain, will climb' (or hike rather) is my motto on my travels and is more often than not the highlight of any trip.

In July 2014, after going through a significant break-up, I had the opportunity to climb Mount Kilimanjaro with Jules and a team of 14 very special people. I knew that I had to do it. I had to push myself to do something that would take me beyond my personal limits, to be able to focus on something else and to let go of the heartbreak.

Through that eight-day journey, I learnt more about myself than I would have in years of therapy. I made friendships that will last a lifetime. It was undoubtedly one of the toughest things I have ever done. On reaching the summit at dawn, I cried with relief as the sun came up over that beautiful mountain. However, I came down the mountain feeling lighter. I had left all the pain and heartache on top of Kili. Sounds like a cliché I know, yet I truly felt reborn.

That feeling stayed with me for months afterwards. The accomplishment empowered me and gave me a new sense of purpose and direction. I am at my happiest when I am on a peak or a summit. It's my escape. I can breathe. My heart is wide open and I am able to gain perspective and let go of things that burden me.

Whenever I am down or things are not as they should be, I remember that euphoria and relief of reaching the top of Kili, and then, once again, all is good with the world.

I believe there is no better cure for ANY affliction!

Val Wiggett

MOVE, SMILE AND LOOK UP!

Here's some really simple advice and it works. When you are feeling low or need to see things from a different perspective, MOVE, LOOK UP and smile. Go on, try it now, see what I mean! Gaining altitude is a great way to adjust your attitude: hike up a hill, climb up a tree, if you are sat down stand up, stand on your chair, go sit in a rooftop café. In short, elevate your presence and 99 times out of 100 your mood will lift – even when you are knocked out flat on the floor choose to look up at the sun or at the stars at night.

For me there is nothing more calming and powerful than taking a good long walk. Whenever you feel frustrated, fed up, upset or overwhelmed, get up, get out and get walking, it will give you the time and space to regain the right perspective and expand your view of what's possible.

"Wherever you go, there you are."

– Zen proverb

"Wherever you are, you are one with the clouds and one with the sun and the stars you see. You are one with everything. That is more true than I can say, and more true than you can hear."

– Shunryu Suzuki

 **BRIGHT IDEA:**

Time to pause again! Grab your journal and a pen and start writing down a list of places, spaces and things that you do when you need to see things differently. How does travelling, going to different places or doing something different, change the way you see things? Who do you reach out to when you need a new perspective on a situation that is challenging you? What works best for you – do you need to be still (meditate) or moving? Alone or with someone who can throw some new light on the situation?

MOVING COUNTRIES

Moving countries definitely gives you the opportunity to see things differently. Sometimes you can go blind when you have lived in a place for a long time. It takes a move to a new country to be able to see clearly again!

Nicholla was able to see and do things differently after moving from Dubai.

> They say there is 'nowt better than change' and I completely believe it! At the time of the change, it is difficult to see how it will be good but when you can look back in the rear view mirror you can start to see the markers of how change was good for you.
>
> My change was moving countries. I grew up in the UAE and was pretty 'Dubai'ified' in that everyone else lived in the wrong place and I lived in the right and BEST place. That said, when change came our way we embraced it wholeheartedly. I was open to ideas and new opinions yet still held the steadfast rule that Dubai was the right place to be.

We moved to Oman and there I was offered opportunities, ideas and abilities to build and create something amazing! I created a Facebook Group called 'Muscat - where can I find...?' to help the community and myself find what we were looking for. It was a simple concept which I sent out to 11 people. It grew rapidly to become Oman's original and most respected 'go to' Q&A community site. This led to more social media work, opportunities to connect with movers and shakers in Oman, host fashion shows and the opportunity to go on the radio and host a show about mums and kids! All unexpected opportunities that I could never have experienced had we stayed in Dubai!

We left Oman five years later and I had a host of new experiences and ideas! I had built a strong community and made so many connections. It was clear to see that I am a 'people explorer' and totally fascinated by people's stories. I felt 'unDubai'ified' – I looked at Dubai with different eyes and understood there were tonnes of stuff outside of the Dubai bubble. I still love Dubai and always will. I grew up there, however the move allowed me to see things very differently. I unattached myself from what I knew, and experienced something very new in Oman. I now have a podcast show interviewing women entrepreneurs and help people with their social media. I truly believe none of this would have happened had we stayed in Dubai. What I learnt is we can be blinded by being in the same space and we really do need to take a step out of the space we know in order to see if it really is for us and what it can or can't offer us!

Nicholla Henderson-Hall – The Learning Curve

FROM YORKSHIRE TO BULGARIA

My nephew Michael made the move from Yorkshire to Bulgaria, where he felt he was able to see and experience so much more then he could living and working in Yorkshire. I wonder how many other young men and women feel this way and choose to move, and how many others close their eyes and choose to stay...

It was nearing the end of 2011, and for me, I already felt like I was stuck in a rut, going through the same everyday routine. I knew I needed a change, but just didn't know what kind of change – or really where to begin with it. I didn't want to work in a call centre for the rest of my life, for sure, but I didn't have any other kind of prospect lined up for myself. Then again, that's been my entire story. I've never really had a specific plan in mind.

One day, I took it upon myself to quit my job. I had been feeling severely depressed working under such restricting conditions, but I worked around the dark feelings and handed my notice in. Even though I had to work for a further 30 days, the move already felt freeing enough and provided a certain motivation.

So what now? No new job lined up. No idea what to do with my life and feeling uninterested in moving from one office job to another. Speaking personally, I'd always been told, "You have to be employed!" or "You have to do this" or "You need to do it this way."

However, having worked four years in that job, I decided that I no longer wanted to do it the way others wanted me to. I didn't want to have a regular routine from day–to–day. I wanted to live my life in my own way.

Taking control of my own life and future began in March of 2012 when I relocated to Sofia, Bulgaria. I'd visited the capital city in January of the same year for two weeks, and it gave me a whole new glance into how life could be. Things were, and still are, very different here. And I don't just mean in the obvious way, i.e. different language, different traditions, different history. Moving to Sofia brought with it many challenges and broke me out of that regular routine. And I'm still seeing things differently from what I've been accustomed to in England. I'm still presented with new learning experiences and challenges four years later.

It's my feeling that such obstacles wouldn't have been presented to me in England. I had to move out of that comfort zone that I'd been in for 26 years of my life to experience a new and different way of living. Placing myself in Bulgaria – something I did on the spur of the moment – gave me the confidence to say to myself that I can succeed and overcome challenges. Nothing is impossible. Put yourself in a different surrounding, see and experience a new location, visit a different country, and in doing so, construct your life the way that you want to.

Michael Catchpole

Instead of moving around the globe and looking out, you can also look inward to yourself and the people around you, something as simple as making new friends.

MAKE NEW FRIENDS

If a move to another country is not on your agenda there are a few other ways to change the way you see things. If you are looking to bring new thoughts, ideas and perceptions into your life, make an effort to meet with new people and mix with different nationalities. Mix with people who have a totally different mindset, outlook and occupation from you. When you hang out with like-minded people it often means that you experience reinforcement of your own thoughts and beliefs. Spending time with people who have the same or similar beliefs leads to 'groupthink' and 'groupsee'.

I am not suggesting that your current friends are not important to you; just make sure you seek out new and diverse friendships to spice up your life. Being around new people will increase the odds that you experience new ways of thinking; besides, it's good to have your views of the world rocked by a conversation with someone who views life differently from the way you do.

SEEING WITH A BEGINNER'S MIND

If you want to see things differently, imagine seeing through the eyes of a child. Children naturally operate with a beginner's mind; they look at the world as it unfolds with an open mind devoid of judgment. As you get older you tend to lose that openness. Have you ever found yourself constantly making assumptions or judging people or situations based on past experiences? Because of everything we know and all the opinions we have already formed, it's often a challenge to see everything with a fresh pair of eyes.

You can practice having a beginner's mind by going to the same places and be present and open to seeing something new every time. Look at your partner, friend, and parent as if you were looking at them for the very first time. What do you see, what else do you see? Have you ever picked up different lines from a song or words from a movie even though you have heard or seen it many times before? When it comes to safety a beginner's mind is a big plus. Think about checking your climbing gear before you use it, or buddy checks when you go diving. Lack of attention, feeling you know it all or taking things for granted can cause havoc. I am fortunate enough to have been to the Arctic seven times yet every time I go I see, experience and feel something new because I chose to be present instead of assuming that everything is as it was a year ago. A strong wind can change the landscape within minutes – be present to the changes. If you have a "been there, done that mentality" you limit your full experience of life. Be open to everything and attached to nothing. Does being an expert mean you have nothing left to learn or discover? I think not, so keep discovering, learning and growing. Start cultivating an attitude of openness and let go of preconceived ideas about a place, person or object – simply look at them with fresh eyes and notice what you really see... then look again.

*"In the beginner's mind there are many possibilities,
but in the expert's there are few."*

– Shunryu Suzuki

BRIGHT IDEA:

Pause for a moment and think about how you can experience the world through a beginner's mind. You can learn new things at any time if you are willing to be a beginner. Start to notice what you see when you really look at something or someone as if it were the first time you had seen it or them. Jot down any insights in your journal – this is an ongoing practice for you!

*"Discovery consists not in seeking new land,
but in seeing with new eyes."*

– Marcel Proust

WHAT ARE YOU LOOKING AT?

Every day you have the choice to choose what you want to look at and experience. You can change the way you feel by changing what you see, both in your mind and in the physical world. Look at happy pictures, listen to upbeat music, read inspirational books, hang out with fun people. See the funny side of everything, turn off the TV, stop reading gossip magazines – yes, go on a negativity diet! Stop watching and reading the news for one week and see how different you feel. If you are meant to know something you will find out one way or the other, usually by a friend asking if you heard the news about… Some people thrive on bad news and gossip – stay well away from them! If you don't like what you see, change what you are looking at.

SEEING THINGS DIFFERENTLY

It's amazing how people can see and experience the same thing yet view it very differently. I was leading a retreat in Nepal when it started pouring down with rain, then came thunder, lightning and hailstones – how magical! Living in the Middle East we don't get this type of weather so it was a treat. We were due to go out kayaking so had to reschedule it to the following day. I was more than happy to stand on the deck and watch people scurry into their rooms and close all the doors and windows. For some people weather like this is a pain; for me and for the gardens at the lodge we were staying at it was an absolute pleasure! I guess if you were kayaking on the lake at the time you would have seen things differently again! Change your 'oh no' to 'oh wow!'

Is it time to change your spectacles? How about looking at life through more imaginative lenses? Try a telescope or a microscope – they are sure to change the way you see things!

LOOKING FOR THE POSITIVE IN EVERY SITUATION

Have you ever found yourself faced with challenges in your life that initially seemed like a negative event that eventually brought gifts and gains that now cause you to look back on the event as positive? These situations all involve a phenomenon that psychologists refer to as 'reframing' and it's a great way of changing the way you look at something and, thus, changing your experience of it.

Are you looking at the roses or the thorns?

Are you looking at smiling or frowning faces?

Do you see challenges as opportunities or as a crisis?

Do you look for the best or worst in people?

BRIGHT IDEA:

Take a quick look back on all that you have experienced over the last year and note down what came about as a result of the experience: a new job, new relationship, new understanding, a new lease of life. Every experience we have brings a gift or a lesson for us, you just have to look a little deeper and see what it is!

HAKUNA MATATA

Losing your job is often viewed as one of the worst things that can happen to you, especially when it happens unexpectedly at the beginning of a new year as it did for Gamze.

On the first day of 2015, I found myself waking up jobless. It felt like an unexpected New Year resolution someone else had planned for me. Actually this was how I perceived it. Despite everything you hear from others, loss of a job is basically one of those unplanned and unwanted things that can shape your world, but also can transform your personality during the process, surprisingly for the better. I believe everybody's journey of adaptability is unique. But at that stage, there were three simple sentences which struck me. 'You are your own worst enemy. You don't want to move on. You feel comfortable staying stuck on the same page.'

My aftershock journey started by detoxifying my soul, which meant giving sufficient time to my inner being for self-reflection, thinking about all the knowledge and skills I possessed, all the capability I have, digesting the past, letting myself go through all the negative feelings I possibly could experience in this situation. Feelings like pain, abandonment, disappointment, anger, fear and sadness. I wrote and wrote about my emotions, instead of suppressing them, feeling grateful for the past, present and the upcoming future. Gradually I shifted my mind from the psychology of losing something toward the psychology of reconstructing brand new paradigms, new ways of reconnecting with the world, reframing my way of thinking, from isolation to initiative thinking, noticing the infinite possibilities. Carl Jung said, "I am not what happened to me. I am what I choose to become."

I also knew that if I could choose to act with resilience and resourcefulness my new calling would find me – and it did.

I adopted the words I recently learned from Tanzanian and Kenyan friends, 'Hakuna Matata', which means 'No worries for the rest of your days' in Swahili. Instead of being stuck in the last couple of chapters of my life book, I dared to open the next ones.

Gamze Hakli Geray

I AM ANOTHER YOU

I am another you basically means that if you can see something in another person, you recognise it within yourself. If it wasn't within you how would you be able to recognise it? When we judge others as being impatient, opinionated, sarcastic, inspirational, courageous or any other trait that we see in them, be it positive or negative, we are actually recognising a part of ourselves. The other person is simply reflecting the elements of you like a mirror. The traits and behaviours which you question or find really annoying in others are often a reflection of your own biggest weaknesses – scary I know! The Mayan expression 'Inlakesh' means 'I am another you'. The next time someone comments on your traits, think about 'Inlakesh' and reflect on how the traits noted exist in both of you at some level or another.

What others do or how they act is their choice, it is up to each of us how we perceive their behaviour. You will see in people whatever you unconsciously expect to see and you will only see, think and feel things that you already have in you. When your assessment of the person standing in front of you comes to your conscious attention, it is more often than not a projection of yourself. Make sure you are giving them a fair chance and consider what it is that you yourself are projecting when other people meet you.

"Everything that irritates us about others can lead us to an understanding of ourselves."

– C. J. G. Jung

SEEING THINGS DIFFERENTLY THROUGH THE FOUR AGREEMENTS

I love the book *The Four Agreements* by Don Miguel Ruiz; if you are not familiar with the book I highly recommend you get a copy or at least look it up online. Once you are familiar with the agreements I can guarantee you will see things very differently. Here they are with a brief explanation from my viewpoint:

1. Be impeccable with your word

   This is the most important agreement yet often the hardest one to follow and keep. Simply put, use your words wisely, honestly and speak with integrity. If you say you are going to do something do it; speak words of kindness, truth and love to yourself and others; take responsibility for your words – the ones you say in your mind and the ones you speak. Know that your words have the power to create or destroy, to keep peace or cause a war so choose them wisely. Stop gossiping or bad mouthing others – it's a waste of energy. If you have something to say, say it to the person that can do something about it and before you say it consider if it's the truth, necessary or beneficial to the situation. When you make a promise to yourself or someone commit to it. If you can't commit then say so. Under promise and over deliver. I have learnt to be pickier about what I say yes to these days. In the past I had a tendency to over commit and spread myself too thinly and then suffer as a consequence. If you want love be loving, if you want kindness be kind, if you want to know the truth, speak the truth. Most of all let go of any words that disempower you or make you feel anything less than the amazing human being that you are.

2. Don't take anything personally

It takes a lot of inner strength not to take things personally. The sooner you realise that what other people say and do is more often a projection of their own reality on you the better. Taking things personally means that you agree with what someone said about you or a situation, it pushes your hot buttons and you react by being defensive or trying to prove a point – you are right and they are wrong, needless to say this creates conflict. When you know what they say isn't true it won't impact you, you are immune to their stories and projections, not your monkey, not your circus. Everyone has different values, morals, ethics and belief systems depending on their experiences and how they see the world so make a concentrated effort not to let what people say, think and do impact you personally – this takes practice. I have found this agreement useful when approaching sponsors for projects, in the past I used to take a "no" personally until I figured out that they were saying no to the project – not to me personally, big difference!

3. Don't make assumptions

By communicating clearly and asking questions you can save yourself a lot of heartache and misunderstanding. I am still a work in progress when it comes to asking or saying what I really want so unless you are a mind reader it can be a bit of a challenge. In business, life and especially in relationships, it's better to ask questions rather than make assumptions. I remember my nephew Michael coming to visit me in Dubai many years ago, at the time I was single and a few people who saw me out and about with him assumed he was my new boyfriend. When I am doing research for expeditions I ask lots of questions, to my clients and to my ground handlers. Just imagine what could happen if I assumed that everyone had the right gear, had done the training and knew where to meet without clear instructions. Ask questions until you are clear.

4. Always do your best

Do the best that you can with the resources and information you have at the time; when you have more information and resources do your best again – no more, no less. I am most productive in the mornings so I make the most of this time. When you are thinking, eating, moving and sleeping well you are much more likely to feel good and do better than when you are tired, hungry, stressed and feeling sluggish. Know when to rest and when to forge ahead. When you are going through significant emotional experiences, low on funds, short on time, do the best you can do at the time, knowing that all things will pass and sooner or later you can and will do better. By taking action – however small it is, you will do better each time. Deciding to take a duvet day is an action – do your best to relax, recover and recharge. When you do your best consistently you become the master of your destiny. Do your best and watch the magic happen.

When you make a conscious effort to live by these four agreements your life will transform. I am not saying it is easy to keep them – nothing great is easily achieved. Just know that they are always there for you. When you slip into old habits or get dragged into somebody else's dramas take three deep breaths and remind yourself of the agreements.

ZOOMING OUT

Having spent time in the Arctic and Antarctica I can hold my hand on my heart and say that being in such vast open spaces gives you a totally different perspective on life. I am lucky to have experienced views from the summit as well as experiencing the vastness of the Polar regions. The sense of 'I' being the most important thing on the earth slips away and you find yourself in an equally spacious, egoless mind. What you think is important is no longer important, you become a small speck in the universe.

By zooming out instead of zooming in, what you see as your internal challenges often fade into insignificance. Mountains become molehills. By distancing yourself from your everyday life you begin to see other people and situations in the world with a more expanded sense of clarity. I know it's not easy to drop everything and just go to the Arctic or Antarctica (if you would like to please drop me a line!) so think of other places or spaces in your mind that you can go that would give you a similar feeling of vastness. Maybe it's a deep meditative state or somewhere that takes you away from a very small perspective to a panoramic wide-angled view. Sometimes just going to dinner by yourself, going to a museum, an art exhibition or any type of creative class can also give you new insights into how to handle something that is currently challenging you.

INTROSPECTION AND SOLUTIONS IN LONELY PLACES

Introspection and soul-searching in lonely places gives you the time and space to look within yourself. There is a big difference between solitude and loneliness, between being alone and feeling lonely. Getting the right balance between time spent alone and time spent with others is a lifelong lesson. Have you ever been to a party and felt lonely despite being surrounded by people? There are times when you will have no desire for social interaction and crave space and solitude to relax and empty your mind of its mental clutter. When you find this space you will not feel lonely even though you are alone. I intuitively know when I want to be surrounded by people and engaged in lively conversation and I know when I need to be quiet, alone and in vast open spaces. The gift of time with yourself, with others, and in nature creates an important magical mix for new insights to unfold.

Vast open spaces allow you to rise above or move away from your current context, widen your perspective and come up with new solutions. They are free of the usual multitude of distractions of everyday life and assist in bringing back a sense of focus to what matters most. They offer time and space for deep reflection, self-renewal and relief from the stress and strains of life in the city. Away from the noise of the city you can contemplate life's big questions and experience the restorative power of Mother Nature. Relaxing into "nothingness" is very powerful. I love floating face down in the ocean with my mask and snorkel on, sensing the gap between my outgoing and incoming breath, treasuring the empty moments of the experience, no sense of direction, just being in a vast ocean where anything is possible. Here I am a floating body of pure potential, where "no thing or no one" disturbs my peace. Where do you need to be right now? Alone, with others or in nature? Simply locking the bathroom door, lighting candles and soaking in a hot tub can be the answer for you. P.S. I love soaking in the bath and taking mental vacations.

Solitude is associated with improved awareness, concentration and creative expression, think about writers, painters, musicians and artists who retreat to special places to create new material. Corporate retreats are very popular now. I love setting them up for clients as they allow teams to step out of the normal work environment and come up with new ideas and solutions to challenges. Instead of phones ringing, birds are singing, minds are open, new insights flow, log cabins, tents, beach huts, and vast open spaces replace concrete walls and air conditioning. Casual clothes replace the city "suited and booted" look – how liberating!

When I come back from trips to the Arctic and Antarctica or the mountains I still find it challenging to re-adjust to the city. The first time I came back from the Arctic I was like a bear with a sore head; cars instead of huskies, walls and buildings instead of mountains and valleys; so much noise after so much silence. The best antidote is to plan another trip!

My good friend Mark, who heads up Outward Bound Oman, has also spent plenty of time in the great outdoors and, like myself, values the importance of spending time in remote places to see things differently and focus on solutions.

"I tell you, deliverance will not come from the rushing, noisy centers of civilization; it will come from the lonely places."

– Fridtjof Nansen

Norwegian explorer, diplomat and humanitarian 1861-1930

How increasingly relevant are the words of one of history's greatest explorers and thinkers; from his extraordinary journeys on the Fram, Nansen knows better than most the value of slowness. We all need time to think, to re-evaluate and take stock, but in today's wired world of data overload and 24/7 connectivity, finding uninterrupted time to reflect is increasingly difficult, yet more needed than ever.

Time spent in the wild, lonely places where mobile phones don't ring, and there are no doors to hide behind, be it in the desert on the edge of Dubai, or the polar wastes, is never wasted. Those wild places have played an integral part in shaping my life; from recreating Nansen's 1888 crossing of the Greenland Ice Cap, to completing a 55-day solo kayak journey from Musandam to Yemen, and more recently an 80-day camel journey from Salalah to Muscat in Oman. When challenged to devise a programme to address the polarisation of cultures and inspire the next generation of global leaders, it was to the desert wilderness of Oman that we turned to create the powerful initiative known as The University of the Desert.

As Nansen intimated, the great thinkers in time, and the solutions, have come from the wild places. My most intense exposure to wild places was an entire year spent living in a small tent, including four months of total darkness some 500 miles from the North Pole on Svalbard, an environment where human beings are not top of the food chain. In early November, just as the sun had risen above the southern horizon for the last time until March, we were paid a visit by the Governor's helicopter. Amongst several months' mail were some newspapers, and two months after the event we must have been some of the last people on the planet to see images of the chaos and atrocity that was 9/11.

What on earth was going on in those rushing, noisy centres of civilisation to the south? Today, more than ever, society needs people to go to those wild places, to reflect, say 'time out' and to come up with those much needed solutions for the future.

Mark Evans MBE, Outward Bound Oman

BRIGHT IDEA:

Pick a few hours, a day, a weekend or longer that you can dedicate to you and you alone in a completely different environment from your everyday life. Distance yourself from everything that you normally see and go somewhere you will not be distracted by people, cars, or buildings. Go to a quiet space in a local park, to the beach, to the forest – anywhere you will not be distracted. Only take bare necessities to include your journal, a pen, water, snacks, and toiletries if you plan to stay overnight. Open the doors of perception and take a long walk...

- Walk mindfully in your new environment

- Ask for insights/guidance

- Notice the sights, sounds and smells that you sense (come to your senses)

- Focus on one question that you would like to answer and trust that the answer will come

- Write down any answers and what you have experienced in your journal

Answers are everywhere if you take the time to be alone and be curious enough to look in unusual places. With the answers and your inner mountain of resources you can **MOVE MOUNTAINS**.

You know the routine now…

1. **MEDITATE**

2. **COME TO YOUR SENSES**

3. **AFFIRMATION**
   I Can See Clearly Now

4. **POWER OF THREE**

What are you going to start, stop and continue doing as a result of reading this chapter?

What's your 'YOU HAVE TO CHANGE WHERE YOU ARE TO SEE THINGS DIFFERENTLY' STORY?

Write it now.

What are you excited, committed and grateful about in relation to this chapter? Jot your thoughts down in your journal or on the Notes pages at the end of the book – and then move on to the next chapter!

RIDE WITH
THE CHANGE

CHAPTER 7

COWGIRL UP

"Worry is like a rockin' horse. It's something to do that don't get you nowhere."

– Old West proverb

ALICE

My late mother-in-law, Alice, introduced me to the expression 'cowgirl up'. The first time I met her I sensed she didn't have a lot of time for anyone who fell into the 'poor me', 'victim' or 'worrier' category, to include her own children. She would listen and discuss the challenge being experienced, offer a couple of suggestions, but never tell you what to do outright. Instead she would look you straight in the eye with a smile and say 'cowgirl up', which pretty much meant know that I am always here for you, but it's up to you to get back on your horse and ride.

When I feel myself slipping into worry mode about something or someone, I think of Alice and start focusing on solutions. Sometimes I even put my cowboy hat on while I think about the best way to handle a situation! This might sound a strange thing to do, just know it's not the only thing I do when I am faced with a challenge!

When faced with a challenge give yourself some space, go for a long walk alone to clear your head, have a discussion with someone who has faced and overcome the same or similar challenge, decide on what you want to do, do it and keep moving forward. Challenges will come and go throughout your life, yet life is too short to stay stuck in worry mode. At the end of the day, whatever lightens your load, allows you to see things differently or gives you the ability to get back on track is much better than inaction. When you fall off your horse, pick yourself up, dust yourself off, focus on what's important to you and get back into the saddle.

When something falls apart often it means something much better is coming together.

"We think that the point is to pass the test or overcome the problem, but the truth is that things don't really get solved.

They come together and they fall apart.

Then they come together again and fall apart again. It's just like that.

The healing comes from letting there be room for all of this to happen: room for grief, for relief, for misery, for joy."
– Pema Chodron

LIFE'S TOUGHEST LESSONS

Heartbreak, loss of a loved one, health issues, empty pockets and the feeling of failure are perhaps five of life's hardest lessons yet paradoxically some of our greatest teachers. From time to time you are thrown off your horse, blown off your mountain, thrown in at the deep end and pushed with your back to the wall. Lost in a maze, weighed down by heavy emotions, looking for a way to get back on your feet, to swim, to move, to let go of the heavy weight you are carrying and find your way again. Sometimes you can do this yourself, you reach a tipping point, a pain threshold, a realisation that your life cannot go on like this anymore… where it is more painful to not do anything than it is to do something about the situation. It takes tough love to get moving towards a solution.

TOUGH LOVE

When you find yourself stuck and metaphorically blind, deaf, dumb and paralysed to what needs to be done, it can take a 'tough love' conversation with a friend, teacher, partner, work colleague or therapist – anyone who can see, hear and sense so clearly what needs to be done – to shift you from 'analysis paralysis' and encourage you to dig deep into your inner mountain of resources and get moving again.

Eventually you find the lesson in the loss, you count your blessings instead of your burdens, you choose to change what you are focusing on, you get back on your horse, back in the game, back to life. Minute by minute, day by day, week by week, month by month you begin to wake up again – to see, hear and sense that you have so many opportunities to move on, knowing that some days the moves will be small and others they will be quantum leaps. What are perceived as negative emotions can actually be our greatest teachers.

"Feelings like disappointment, embarrassment, irritation, resentment, anger, jealousy, and fear, instead of being bad news, are actually very clear moments that teach us where it is that we're holding back.

They teach us to perk up and lean in when we feel we'd rather collapse and back away. They're like messengers that show us, with terrifying clarity, exactly where we're stuck.

This very moment is the perfect teacher, and, lucky for us, it's with us wherever we are."

– Pema Chodron

BRIGHT IDEA:

Pause for a moment and think about the times in your life where you have felt stuck and unable to handle a situation. How did you snap out of it? Grab a pen and your journal and note down the situation, what was the tipping point, what did you do to get moving again? Who helped you get moving? What inner resources did you draw on to overcome the challenge? What did this teach you about yourself?

PICKING UP THE PIECES

I have had my fair share of situations that have brought me to tears and I am sure there will be many more as the years pass by. Tears of relief, joy, sadness and laughter. I often think that when you lie down face up and your tears start running into your ears it's a way of clearing out your eyes and ears so you can see and hear what you really need to and make a clean start. Clean starts give you the opportunity to pick up the pieces you want to keep hold of and create a new mosaic of your life.

Remember the serenity prayer…

Grant me the serenity to accept the things I cannot change

The courage to change the things I can

And the wisdom to know the difference

PADDLE UP AND SADDLE UP

Remember the story in chapter one about my visit to Malaysia where I first saw Mount Kota Kinabalu and the boat races at the Sarawak Regatta? A little history for you – the Regatta is an annual event held on the Sarawak River in Kuching. Kuching is also known as Cat City so when you go look out for the big statues of cats overlooking the water front. The Regatta traces it origins to the era of Sir James Brooke, a British adventurer whose exploits in Malaysia led to him being the White Rajah of Sarawak. Sir James instituted the use of boat races to settle conflict between the tribes in Sarawak.

The next story I have to share is a good river "cowgirl up" story. No conflicts to solve, just balmy weather to contend with!

I put the call out for women and men to join me in Sarawak and managed to persuade five people to say "yes" to the adventure of racing a longboat up the river. We combined forces with a local team from the Tourism Malaysia office to make up a boat of 20 paddlers for the 1500m race. Our race was scheduled for Sunday at 2pm so we spent Saturday watching the other teams race and getting a few practice sessions in with our new team mates. The weather had been fabulous so far and we were looking forward to our debut on the river. Race time approached and we paddled to the start line ready for action. Paddles at the ready, heads down, waiting for the fog horn to sound... time to get moving! We had only been paddling 5 minutes when something quite extraordinary happened. The sun totally disappeared behind dark heavy clouds; rain, thunder, lightning and winds of Biblical proportions swept around us... not quite the race conditions we expected or had trained for!

Several boats capsized in the storm leaving team members stranded in the river holding on to their paddles and trying to retrieve their boat. Our boat was a little broader and deeper so we miraculously managed to stay afloat. A few of our paddles snapped under the pressure of the raging river leaving some of us with just a shaft of wood in our hands. No need for sunglasses now, we needed windscreen wipers on them. For the most part we had no idea where we were heading as the wind blew our boat from left to right "snaking" along the river. We kept going against all odds and after what seemed a lifetime on the river we finally crossed the finish line to the roars of the crowds and dignitaries in the VIP box. Exhausted and dripping wet we stepped out of the boat, onto the jetty and, with heads held high and paddles in hand, walked to the podium where, despite the fact that we came in last, the Minister of Tourism presented us with a large wooden model of a hornbill (the hornbill is the national bird of Sarawak). He congratulated us on our achievement, thanked us for being the first foreigners from the Middle East to take part in the races and said, "please come back next year".

I vowed to return with a full team from Dubai and managed to fulfil the promise three years later by taking a group of 20 women known as the "Beyond Expectations" team to race in the International Tourist category.

We trained together on anything we could get our hands on; improvising quite a bit as longboats were not available in Dubai. We had to settle for steel barrel rafts, Canadian canoes, and kayaks – anything to get on the water and paddle. Instead of worrying about what we didn't have we focused on what we could do and combined time on the water with circuit training and regular pep talks encouraging the team to visualise our success and imagine being on a longboat racing through the finish line.

Being the first and only team of women from the UAE to take part in the race we were able to get plenty of media attention making it easier to secure sponsorship from Malaysia Airlines for our flights and Land Rover for our team kit. We were lean, clean paddling machines and had set our sights on living up to our team name of going Beyond Expectations... and that's exactly what we did, bringing home silver medals and plenty of wild stories from our time in Sarawak.

Wherever there is a woman's will there is always a way. I have never ceased to be amazed at the determination, hardiness and resourcefulness of women despite what they might be going through at the time, which leads me into Billie's account of her experience as one of the twenty women who raced beyond expectations.

Picking up a paddle helped Billie pick up the pieces of her life and get moving again.

With a painful divorce behind me, losing my estranged father before saying goodbye, a business in tatters, four teenage children and 40 years on this earth I didn't exactly feel on top of the world. Zero confidence, low self-esteem, no self-belief, awful body image issues, not to mention the inner pain and turmoil that had brought me to my knees. I was a wreck and in insecurity overload, feeling worthless and a failure. I was at a fork in the road to either take the right path and change my attitude or the left path and take the road to nowhere.

Physically I was not in bad shape, had worked out three times a week, but was nowhere near the condition I wanted to be in. I needed inspiration to keep fighting to be motivated and to have a spiritual therapist to engage me in a more positive frame of mind. Julie Lewis, a few oil barrels welded together and 22 women all with different stories to share were to be my saving grace. The journey had begun on our first meeting – to be the first all-woman team of expats to race in the Sarawak regatta. I knew I had to go, it was as if it had been written in the sand. My father had been a soldier in the British army in Borneo and as a child I had the pleasure of looking at old black and white photographs listening to his encapsulating stories of the Iban tribes with their stretched ears, decorative tattoos, their longhouses and communities of savages and head hunters. The beauty of the rivers, untouched jungles and the Orangutan monkeys high in the tree tops. It was always on my bucket list, however I did not expect to go there as an athlete and beat the men's Singapore national team and come second in an international sporting event.

Our training was intense in the Dubai summer heat, scorching sands, 5am starts – mothers, daughters, teachers, business women all astride oil barrels on the crystal clear waters of Jumeirah Beach. We trained hard, had a few dropouts but the ones who survived went on to experience a soul-changing journey and friendships that would be solidified and last a lifetime.

It was truly an emotional experience that changed my life and taught me how I was supposed to be and not to revel in self-pity.

This cowgirl wasn't riding a horse but had mounted up and saddled up to the beauty of her life with paddles at the ready!

Billie Mobayed

COWGIRL UP INDIANA JONES STYLE!

Sometimes however much you plan and prepare, the universe has some surprises planned for you; this was very much the case for the *Jewels of Arabia* challenge in 2007. Whatever could go wrong did go wrong; that said, a lot of things did go to plan. We all managed to rise to the occasion – cowgirl up and Indiana Jones style! Jo recounts the adventure…

October 2007, I find myself on Jules's 'Jewels of Arabia – Indiana Jones style adventure' driving across Wadi Rum, Jordan in a Land Rover convoy, fulfilling a dream – to go on a proper, real 'grown-up' adventure – 'Be careful what you wish for Jo!'

The Land Rovers coming from Dubai got detained at the Saudi Border; one of our team members didn't make it due to visa issues; we had storms of Biblical proportions that Jordan hadn't seen in the longest time, we were swept out of our tents, quite literally; we climbed a mountain (apparently it was a small one as mountains go, but I am claiming I summited a mountain :-) where one of our party slipped and broke her ankle; a member of my team locked the keys in our Land Rover with all of our luggage in and no spare until later the next day; my roomie/tent partner suffered food poisoning; I could go on...

We sourced a new set of 4x4s in Jordan, we chased goats across Wadi Rum and my team almost sold me for camels to a local Bedouin (I hoped they were joking :-). We bonded over hot tea in the middle of the darkest, stormiest, scariest night huddled together in the main tent, as our marvellous guides bravely repaired holes that had appeared in the canvas. We rescued and convoyed one of our team members with the broken ankle to hospital. I was offered clothes and toiletries from the other ladies while mine were locked in the car; we danced in the desert while waiting for blow-outs on tyres to be fixed; we cried, we laughed, we cared for each other and we bonded. We got our treasure from Indiana himself in Petra – or did we? The real treasure came from that which was inside each and every one of us, individually and collectively. I have fantastic memories and friends for life and I had a proper, real 'grown-up' adventure.

It really is all about how you choose to perceive events, the attitude you take and how you really embrace everything that life brings your way. I invite you to 'Go there!' Go to those places that feel a little scary, take a risk and choose to take the positive from every situation you face. To bounce back after each and every fall. The richness and rewards you will gain as a result are priceless. Cowgirl up!

Jo Simpson, author of The Restless Executive

BOUNCING BACK

The ability to get back into the saddle and step into the adventure of life and love again whatever life throws or has thrown at you is an essential trait of 21st century living in business, sports and life. This bounce-back ability (resilience) starts at an early age. Just think about how many times a baby falls down before she or he finally learns to walk. Every time the baby falls they are supported and encouraged by their parents to get back up and have another go and keep going till they have got it. There is no way you would say 'oh forget it, you'll never be able to walk' to a child, yet as an adult you often give up after just a few tries at something. How many times did you fall off your bike, your horse, your skateboard, your skis, or your snowboard before you finally got it?

Merriam-Webster defines resilience as, "the ability to become strong, healthy, or successful again after something bad happens". A second definition is, "the ability of something to return to its original shape after it has been pulled, stretched, pressed or bent". How many times have you felt "pulled out of shape" or have experienced setbacks, stress, disappointments, misfortune, change or illness? They are all part of life's rich tapestry of experiences so how do you weave in and out of them and show up stronger, wiser and develop your bounce-back ability? Think about Thomas Edison's words, "I have not failed. I have just found 10,000 ways that don't work" or Eleanor Roosevelt's, "A woman is like a tea bag; you never know how strong it is until it's in hot water".

You develop resilience as a direct result of your life experiences. The more resilient you are the better your ability is to adapt to change and growth. The good news is that it's a quality you can learn to cultivate. A certain amount of challenge can actually be a good thing. When I was 11 years old I went to a private Quaker school in West Yorkshire as a boarder. This meant leaving home and sleeping in a dormitory with twenty complete strangers... who, I hasten to add, eventually became best friends. The first few weeks were a big challenge for me; I made reverse charge calls to my parents every other day asking to come home! "It will get better and if you feel the same way at the end of term we can talk about it again". When this was not enough to convince me, Dad would drive over for a pep talk, more often than not we sat outside the Brown Cow, a local pub with picnic benches out front. A bag of crisps, a Coke and a tough yet reassuring talk worked, so off I went back to school believing that things could only get better – and they did!

Day by day it became easier to be away from home and develop a new tribe to hang out with – so much so that by the end of the second term I often chose not to go home and took the opportunity to spend time visiting my friends' families or going on sports training camps. I stayed on as a boarder until I was 18. My claim to fame is being Head Girl in the final year, it seems the character building years and resilience paid out dividends in the end.

This early departure from home obviously stood me in good stead for travelling around the globe, being able to mix with people from all walks of life and enjoy expatriate life… and come to think of it, being able to sleep in mountain huts beside complete strangers sharing the same passion as myself for reaching new heights! Taking the rough with the smooth, means learning from every experience. Sometimes life sucks – you lose your job, your partner, your dog, or you're low on funds. Acknowledge such times, focus on what you can do, reach out for help and know you are not the only person in the world to experience these challenges. More often than not it means something or someone better is coming along. Eventually you will find the positive in even the gloomiest of situations. For every no there is a yes waiting for you – keep going until you get to it.

Rather than lose yourself in a story of despair, change your story to one of courage and success. Change starts with you, nobody can rescue you until you are prepared to rescue yourself. Be your own hero, ask for help when you need it and be prepared to repair and reweave your personal and professional tapestry of life to the work of art it is meant to be.

Be optimistic and hopeful instead of pessimistic and hopeless. Be courageous instead of being discouraged. See challenges as opportunities to learn and grow. Most of all please promise me that you will put self-care and nurturing activities first and foremost. This means lots of time in nature, plenty of exercise, meditation, focusing on solutions, eating healthy food, getting quality sleep, being comfortable with who you are, talking things out with a friend or therapist, finding your "tribe", focusing on what brings you joy and having plenty of interests outside of work and home. Select one or more of these to implement daily and stick to them consistently so they become a habit. Over time you will see incredible benefits and will be much more able to bounce back.

> *"Our greatest glory is not in never falling, but in rising up every time we fall."*
>
> – Confucius

STARTING OVER

J.K. Rowling said, "Rock bottom is the solid foundation on which I built my life." When you have hit rock bottom, the only way is up... and it's up to you to get moving. Starting over is one of the toughest things you can do. Starting over can represent exciting new beginnings, these are usually the ones you have chosen and planned for yourself such as moving to a new country, starting a new job, an educational course or a new diet and exercise regime. Other 'start overs' can come without much warning and be totally overwhelming. It could be the unexpected loss of a loved one, being let go from your job or having to leave your home or country at short notice.

When Iraq invaded Kuwait in 1990 I was forced to make a decision whether to stay or make a move. The thought of being rounded up and taken to Baghdad didn't appeal to me so three weeks into the occupation I escaped across the desert with a group of people with just a small bag and my passport in hand. We were able to reach the Saudi border and after several strained conversations I finally made it to the British Embassy in Riyadh where I was able to call my parents, let them know I was alive and that I needed some cash to get a flight home. They transferred money through the Foreign Office and a day later I was on a plane flying back to the UK. Once home I called the head office of the hotel chain I had been hired by to let them know I had deserted my post, could be contacted on my parents' number and that I was more than happy to be re-located to a new job.

Finding a new posting at the level I wanted with the same hotel chain proved to be a challenge so it was time to knock on other doors, put my CV out there and network. Within one month I had a new job as a Country Club Manager in Cheshire giving me a stable income, a new focus, a new set of work colleagues and plenty of positive distractions after the harrowing experience of fleeing Kuwait. Starting over in the UK after living in the Middle East brought challenges of its own, yet at the same time it provided a new foundation to build a new life. Four years later I moved back to the Middle East and know that, if needs must, I can move and make the best of most situations based on my Kuwait experience.

Another "starting over" story that springs to mind is when Calin and I moved to Hong Kong. At the time we were living in Dubai and the construction industry was experiencing a major downturn. Many companies were letting staff go at short notice. During this time period Calin called me and asked if I wanted to go to Hong Kong. I thought he was hinting at a trip for the Rugby Sevens then swiftly realised he meant to go to live and work there. Two weeks later his company transferred him to work on projects in Hong Kong. I followed two months later, registered Mountain High Asia as a business and got stuck into building a name for myself in a whole new market. The move and transition was not without its challenges yet it opened up a whole new world of opportunities and friendships. Even though we only stayed there for two years before returning to the Middle East we both made the most of the unexpected move and know that when future moves unfold we have plenty of experience in moving with them. The one thing I can tell you is that you are never really stuck. You might be terrified of change, feel cornered or held back by your current situation yet I want you to know that starting over is possible. Re-invent yourself, take a break , revisit your goals, network like your life depends on it, knock on doors, remove everything from sight that keeps you stuck, distract yourself, get educated, quit any bad habits, vent to a friend, focus on solutions, start journaling, pick up old hobbies or start new ones. The only way you will be disappointed is if you never even try; it's never too late to get started – it's only too late when you die. Accept what has happened, get moving and always think UP instead of down.

When life knocks you off your horse the best thing to do is get back on as soon as you can and keep riding. That's exactly what Dr Oudi did when his father died unexpectedly.

> In 2004 my dream came true when I opened my clinic in Toronto, Canada. In my eyes, I was living on-purpose and living large. Everything changed in an instant however when my father suffered a heart attack in the reception area of my clinic. Dad made it into the operating room, but never made it out.

With a devastated mother who was deteriorating right before my eyes, I made a heartfelt decision. I put a little money in my pocket, love in my heart and put family first. I sold everything I had in 60 days, ultimately gave away my clinic and started over in Dubai. With no job, no job offer and being virtually broke, you could say I hit rock bottom. Now 11 years later, at 42 years of age, I am living large again.

In his own words, here's how he got moving.

I believe so strongly in the following:

1. *The purpose of your heart is to house your purpose. Your mind needs to mind its business and let your heart lead the way.*

2. *The purpose of your mind is to overcome obstacles. Welcome obstacles, don't run.*

3. *The purpose of your body is to be the vehicle of your dream. Take care of it.*

4. *The purpose of your voice is to speak to both serve and sell, to both stand up to people and express your appreciation to them.*

I woke up each morning, took my highest, most important steps. I got my mind, body and voice working for me instead of against me. If you do the same, I know you can get back on your horse and ride.

Dr Oudi Abouchacra, Inspired Results

WHEN THE YOGHURT HITS THE FAN

Some people are better at coping with challenges than others; they are able see the silver lining of every cloud and bounce back from tough times even stronger than before. The adage 'seven times you fall, eight times you rise' comes to mind.

Whatever stage or age you are in your life right now, it's smart to develop your resilience (bounce-back factor). The yoghurt can hit the fan anytime, any place, anywhere, it's how you deal with it that counts. There are many great books on resilience so I will keep this section short; in a nutshell, resilient people are:

- Optimistic

- Calm in a crisis

- Good at finding solutions and solving problems

- Confident

- Self-reliant yet willing to ask for help

- Able to keep their head

- Have a positive mental attitude

- Trust their intuition

- See the silver lining of every cloud

- Don't take things personally

- Know how to handle and manage stress

- Good at making decisions

- Never give up!

I love the quote below from the film *The Best Exotic Marigold Hotel*. How about posting it on a note and sticking it on your bathroom mirror, office noticeboard, or in your wallet:

> *"Everything will be alright in the end, so if it is not alright it is not the end."*
>
> – Deborah Moggach

My dad is a big reader and would often share passages, poems and quotes from books that he was reading at the time. One poem that I remember to this day is the legendary poem *If* by Rudyard Kipling. We were encouraged to learn it off by heart as children and to this day it is still one of my 'go to' resources – I just change the last few words to 'you'll be a woman my daughter'!

IF

If you can keep your head when all about you

Are losing theirs and blaming it on you,

If you can trust yourself when all men doubt you,

But make allowance for their doubting too;

If you can wait and not be tired by waiting,

Or being lied about, don't deal in lies,

Or being hated, don't give way to hating,

And yet don't look too good, nor talk too wise:

If you can dream – and not make dreams your master;

If you can think – and not make thoughts your aim;

If you can meet with Triumph and Disaster

And treat those two impostors just the same;

If you can bear to hear the truth you've spoken

Twisted by knaves to make a trap for fools,

Or watch the things you gave your life to, broken,

And stoop and build 'em up with worn-out tools:

If you can make one heap of all your winnings

And risk it on one turn of pitch-and-toss,

And lose, and start again at your beginnings

And never breathe a word about your loss;

If you can force your heart and nerve and sinew

To serve your turn long after they are gone,

And so hold on when there is nothing in you

Except the Will which says to them: 'Hold on!'

If you can talk with crowds and keep your virtue,

Or walk with Kings – nor lose the common touch,

If neither foes nor loving friends can hurt you,

If all men count with you, but none too much;

If you can fill the unforgiving minute

With sixty seconds' worth of distance run,

Yours is the Earth and everything that's in it,

And – which is more – you'll be a woman, my daughter!

I wonder if Kipling had heard the 'cowgirl up' expression when he wrote this!

TAKING 100% RESPONSIBILITY

Masters take 100% responsibility for their lives; instead of asking 'why' questions they ask 'how, what, where, who and when' questions. Masters choose to change a frown to a smile, to live and act by their values, to be the best they can be and step into their personal power yet still have the humility to laugh at themselves when things don't quite go to plan. They experience all their emotions yet do not get stuck in them; they choose to focus on solutions instead of repeating what the challenge is; they have the courage to ask 'What needs to happen here?' instead of holding their hands up in the air and saying 'Why is this happening?'

When things go wrong having a good vent might feel therapeutic; however, making a habit of it and venting too long, drains your energy levels and doesn't actually solve the problem. Instead of repeating your gripes to those around you, practise acceptance and start taking action to resolve the situation.

I have learnt (sometimes the hard way!) that it's best not to resist challenges when they come, resisting them holds you to them. Whatever you resist persists until you have the courage to face it head on. For example, difficult conversations or things that are niggling you with loved ones or work colleagues that get put off for fear of rocking the boat can later cause a metaphorical Tsunami. I've learnt that it's better to speak up straight away if things are not right. Cowgirl up!

RIDE WITH THE CHANGE

Whatever you have faced or are facing, know that it will pass.

A butterfly is safe in its cocoon yet it will never reach its full potential by staying there. Getting out of the cocoon is challenging yet in the process of coming out the butterfly develops its wings and can start to fly. As humans we have a tendency to resist change rather than embrace it. We are afraid of the possible outcomes and more often than not view change as being disruptive to our stability or security. We live in a world of changes so it pays to get used to them. The seasons change, our minds change, technology, policies, markets, weather, prices, fashion... you name it and it changes. What worked last week, last month or last year can change in an instant. Think of all the new technology and software innovations and updates that make a task safer, easier or twice as fast to complete. Think about how Skype has changed the way we communicate. When I first changed from a PC to a MAC it was a challenge getting used to it at first, now I can't imagine going back to a PC! Can you imagine wearing something you wore 10 years ago, listening to the same music, going to the same places and never ever trying anything new? Instead of whining about change, look for the good in it, grow and learn to make the most of it.

I know it sounds like a cliché yet it is so true. Nothing stays the same forever. Change is one of the few constants in life and, as the saying goes, the only person that doesn't mind change is a baby with a wet nappy. Often we have quite a resistance to change, it helps to know and believe that when something big changes in your life, something better is coming, so ride with the change.

BRIGHT IDEA:

When you find yourself repeatedly thinking and talking about your challenges, STOP. Instead focus all your energy on solutions. Take a break now, grab your journal and write down all the possible solutions to any current challenges or big changes you are experiencing, keep asking yourself: What else, what else? Whatever comes into your head write it down, keep writing until you come up with a solution that works for you and helps you ride with the change.

GUT FEELINGS

There will always be plenty of people around you, well-meaning friends and family, who out of their love and concern for you might be telling you what they think you should do and how you should do it. They may well have some good advice, however it's your life and I am confident that you know yourself better than anyone else. Don't be afraid to ask for help from someone whose opinion and insights you value, someone who won't be offended even if you don't end up taking their advice. It's important to practise listening to your inner mountain, your 'gut feelings' and do what sits right with you based on the information you have at the time – knowing that if you need to make changes later you can course-correct.

Most of you will have experienced the sense of knowing something before you knew it. Gut feelings are intuitive hunches or insights that often defy logic. When something feels wrong in your body you are the first to sense it, you can sense when you are in danger, when someone is following you, looking at you, or needs help. It could be as simple as driving home from work and getting a sudden urge to take the highway instead of your usual route then find out later that there was a flood or major accident on your normal route. I have friends who stuck to their guts when they felt something was not right even though their doctor said nothing was wrong with them; when they insisted on second and third opinions they finally got to the root of the problem and were able to deal with it rather than let it become a major health issue.

You can read facial expressions and emotional signals in another person almost instantly and just "know what to do". Having travelled extensively I get very strong gut feelings when I need to cross the street, get off the path, jump out of a taxi, or leave a place that just doesn't "feel right". It could be a burning sensation in my stomach, an image that flashes into my mind, tingles in my body, my heart rate increasing or simply an unexplainable certainty and knowing that something is just not right and I need to move. You know when something feels right and when something feels wrong, the aim is to strike the balance between rational thinking and gut instinct. When you follow your gut feelings you will find that life flows more easily; when you go against your gut feelings you tend to find yourself pushing, struggling or forcing things to happen. You can't always hear your intuitive voice, it gets lost in the noise of a multitude of thoughts and activity. One of the quickest and easiest ways to strengthen your intuition is to let go of your "monkey mind" and stop multi-tasking. By clearing your mind and being present you clear away the noise and distractions that can mask your gut feelings.

MORE POWER OF THREE!

In addition to the Power of Three exercise you see at the end of each chapter that asks you to think about what you are going to stop, start and continue doing, I'd like to share another Power of Three ritual with you that will help you stay physically, mentally, spiritually and emotionally in tune so that whatever life throws your way you can 'cowgirl up' with more ease. It's simple and effective so give it a try:

- Free your mind   - meditate

- Energise your body   - move/exercise

- Nurture your spirit of adventure - do something new

  …and drink lots of water.

I have three rocks on my office desk and keep three small ones in my bag as a reminder to do this daily. Go find three rocks now!

Let's round off this chapter with one of my favourite Apache blessings, native American Indians always have plenty of solid advice for cowgirls and cowboys!

May the sun bring you new energies by day

May the moon softly restore you by night

May the rain wash away any worries you have

and the breeze blow new energy into your being,

and then, all the days of your life may you

walk gently through the world

and know its beauty and yours.

Time to switch off again, you know what to do!

1. **MEDITATE**

2. **COME TO YOUR SENSES**

3. **AFFIRMATION**
   I am ready to Cowgirl Up!

4. **POWER OF THREE**

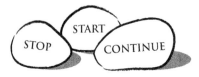

What are you going to start, stop and continue doing as a result of reading this chapter?

What's your 'COWGIRL UP' STORY?

Write it now.

What are you excited, committed and grateful about in relation to this chapter? Jot your thoughts down in your journal or on the Notes pages at the end of the book – and then move on to the next chapter!

BOOST YOUR CHI

CHAPTER 8

WHAT BRINGS YOU JOY GIVES YOU ENERGY

"Nothing is more important than reconnecting with your bliss.
Nothing is as rich. Nothing is more real."

– Deepak Chopra

To move and climb mountains you need energy. No energy – no movement. This chapter will zone in on how to reconnect to your joy and boost your energy so you can handle any challenges you face in life with much more ease – you will be able to move mountains and climb one!

The Oxford dictionary defines joy as *'a vivid emotion of pleasure arising from a sense of well-being'*. As an advocate for health and well-being I like the connection of joy to well-being. When you are seeing, hearing, smelling, tasting and living your joy, you look and feel good; your immune system gets a boost, your energy levels are high and everyone loves to be around you – you are contagious! Yay!

CREATING YOUR JOY LIST

To live a joyful life effortlessly it helps to know what brings you joy, puts a smile on your face, a spring in your step and a sparkle in your eye. In a moment you will start working on your own joy list, here's just a few of mine to get you moving:

- Being in nature

- Walking

- Swimming in the ocean

- Dark chocolate - Lindt Mint Intense please!

- Climbing mountains

- Sitting round a camp fire

- Rolling in the snow

- Laughing

- Smiling and seeing others smile

- Seeing others succeed

- Singing in the car with *Take It Easy* by the Eagles playing out loud

- Watching children play

- Smelling flowers

- Soaking in a bath

- Listening to my niece Alisha sing – a rising star to look out for

- Candles and Buddhas

- Going to bookstores

- Discovering new places

- Learning new things

- Massages

- Watching the sun set and rise

- Moon and star gazing

I am sure you get the idea now! So it's over to you to enjoy the next few exercises.

BRIGHT IDEA:

So now it's your turn. Grab a pen and your journal and write down people, places, activities or things that bring you joy. Do this quickly and without thinking too much. Write everything that comes into your mind, they don't need to take lots of time or cost lots of money; keep adding to this list and make sure you connect with what brings you joy every day for the rest of your life! When you are doing this exercise play some of your favourite music, kick off your shoes and pour yourself a cheeky glass of red wine or a joyful pot of green tea!

YOUR JOY BOARD

In addition to your joy list, I suggest you create a JOY board and cover it with images of everything and everybody that brings you joy. This is a simple yet effective way of bringing your joy to life. Put a picture of yourself in the middle of your board and every time you look at it JUMP FOR JOY. If you prefer to do this in a sketch book that you can carry around with you, go for it; you may prefer to create a JOY board on Pinterest or start a JOY series on Instagram.

To supercharge your joy think of the times when you were feeling happy, brimming with love and energy:

- What were you doing?

- Who were you with?

- Where were you?

- When was the last time you felt like this?

- How can you bring more experiences like this into your life?

- The more you focus on joy, the more joy you attract.

JOY SAPPERS AND ENERGY DRAINERS

It's easy to get caught up in your daily routine and put the things you'd really love to do on hold. When you find yourself lacking energy, foggy brained and uninspired, more often than not it's because you have started to give into life's demands or other people's demands. Have you let your own needs get pushed on to the back burner, maybe doing things you don't even enjoy, or being with people who drain your energy?

Here's a few examples of energy drainers:

- Saying yes when you mean no

- Deflecting compliments

- Overeating and drinking

- Overspending

- Not exercising

- Always putting others first

- Being over accommodating – a people pleaser

- Giving away your personal power

- Taking on everyone's challenges

- Ignoring your deepest desires

- Dismissing your gut feelings

- Not setting healthy personal boundaries

- Comparing yourself to others

- Being in constant stressful situations

- Skipping meals

- Not getting enough sleep

- Over attached to technology

- Little or no connection to people, pets, animals

- Mental obesity – having a hundred thoughts in your head

Any other energy drainers to add to this list – note them down.

If you relate to some of these then STOP! Look at how you are spending your days, who you are spending your time with; look at your joy list and joy board and make sure you start doing something EVERY DAY to reconnect to your joy. This form of self-care ENERGISES YOU. What do you do when your phone is low on battery or your car is low on fuel? You plug in the phone and fuel up the car. What do you do when your joy batteries are low? Make sure it's a healthy balance of rest and reconnection to your joy list – not more cups of coffee!

Give yourself permission NOW to do more things on your joy list, to be with people you love, go to places that make you happy, that put a sparkle back in your eye, fill your body with endorphins and create a deep inner soul smile.

HOW TO SPOT JOYFUL PEOPLE

- They like themselves and see the good in other people

- They are open to life's possibilities

- They hardly ever complain

- They take every day as it comes

- They enjoying giving and receiving

- They are self-reliant

- They look after themselves

- They look on the bright side

- They focus on solutions

- They smile and laugh often

Be one of them.

You have very little to give anyone unless your internal joy is radiating outwards. Joy and sadness cannot exist in the same space at the same time; accept sadness when it shows up, then tap into what brings you joy to get you moving again.

TIME FLIES WHEN YOU'RE HAVING FUN

Have you ever noticed how time flies when you are doing something you love? When you are 'in flow' all your worries seem to disappear, hours pass by in the blink of an eye and before you know it the day has gone. I can spend hours in a bookstore without batting an eyelid; when I am outdoors I can walk for hours in nature without even looking at my watch.

What do you do, where do you go, who are you with when you are 'in the flow zone'? Usually it's something that comes very naturally to you. Do you get lost in music, in books, or creating something? When you are doing what you love, expanding your mind, exercising your body, being with people who share your passion it's very easy to find yourself enjoying what Maslow refers to as 'peak experiences' – our highest state of functioning/self-actualisation. Even if what you are doing is challenging you can keep going all day because you are at one with whatever you are doing. You don't need anyone to motivate you to do it, you are inspired to do it, there is no stopping you!

If, on the other hand, you find yourself wishing time away, clock watching or needing constant external motivation to do something, it's definitely time to move on from what you are doing or delegate it to someone who would love to do it for you!

BOOSTING YOUR CHI

The western world is taking more interest in the human energy field and how important it is to the overall functioning of the mind, body, spirit and emotions. Through the practice and combination of several mind-body disciplines you can create and increase a strong flow of life energy through your body and boost your Chi. The Chinese refer to life's energy force as Chi, Qi or Ki and believe that everything has its own life force. Nature overflows with Chi. Trees, flowers, mountains, oceans, rivers, the sun are all loaded with a powerful positive life force you can tap into daily – free Chi!

There is nothing natural about sitting in an air conditioned office or home under florescent lighting staring at a computer screen for hours on end. This is a very quick way to drain your Chi, yet we all do it. To restore and re-boot your Chi, make sure you get up and get outdoors. Ideally every 90 minutes move away from all technology and take a Chi boost break! If you can't get out into nature, bring nature in to you. Plants, flowers, water features, rocks, images of nature placed in your office and home will all boost your environmental Chi. Unless there is a force 10 storm blowing outside, open all your windows and let Mother Nature's air flow through for an instant Chi fix.

SILENT ENERGY PRACTICES

Spiritual practices like meditation, yoga and pranayama (breathing) also boost your Chi. They all lead to a space of silence which is charged with creative intuitive energy. Often in this zone of silence insights and discoveries are made, poems, songs and ideas for great adventures emerge… so head for your yoga mat and stay there a while.

My personal favourite silent energy practices are *Zazen* – seated meditation and *Kinhin* – walking meditation. Sitting or walking in silence is excellent for focus and discipline; the focus is on just sitting, just breathing, just walking, letting words, ideas and thoughts pass through you without getting involved or holding on to them. Rather than go into great detail here I highly recommend you look these practices up and give them a try. If they resonate with you, incorporate them into your daily life and watch your life transform. Meditation is not just for hippies, monks and artists; top athletes and business leaders meditate to clear and still their minds. If you are a *busy bee* and live your life at 100 miles per hour I highly recommend you stop *buzzing* for 20 minutes every day – be still and silent, or walk mindfully in silence, your mind and body will thank you for it.

CHI BOOSTER TIPS

- Move

- Eat nourishing foods

- Drink more water

- Breathe!

- Laugh

- Smile

- Dance like no one is watching

- Spend more time in nature

- Get a massage every week

- Wear colours that you love

- Get a good night's sleep

- Let go of any negative emotions and replace them with new empowering emotions

- Meditate

- Take up yoga or Tai Chi

- Have an attitude of gratitude

- Spend time with those you love

Add your own Chi boosters to the list above and post them on a note where you can see them to remind you to take Chi booster breaks.

By the way, good sound vibrations also boost your Chi. Sing, listen to music, drum, whistle, play instruments, or simply sit outdoors quietly and listen to the sound of nature, they all emit a vibrational energy into the world – sounds good to me!

SAY CHEESE

Smiling is a simple way to boost your Chi and brings a host of other benefits with it:

- It's contagious – most people will smile with you, back at you

- It lowers your stress and anxiety levels

- Releases endorphins

- Strengthens your immune system

- Makes you look even more gorgeous

- It makes you look younger (yes please!)

Smile and the world smiles with you. Have fun with this and smile at every person you see today and every day onwards.

COMIC RELIEF

There's nothing like a good old belly laugh to lighten things up and bring people together. Everything from a slight giggle to 'I almost peed my pants with laughter' can change your mood and the ambience of a room immediately. One of the prerequisites for coming on a Mountain High expedition or retreat is a positive sense of humour. The ability to laugh at yourself and with others, even when things don't go to plan, makes for a much better experience.

When things are getting too serious, take a giggle break, lighten up and then start to refocus on solutions. In fact, stop reading right now and have a giggle or go and tickle someone, preferably someone you know or you could be in serious trouble! Laughing is your built-in stress reliever and a great way to move you out of life's dramas. It's a free and easy way to lower your blood pressure, reduce your stress hormone levels and trigger the release of endorphins. It's said that, on average, a child laughs about 300 times a day and an adult laughs an average of 17 times a day – time to lighten up methinks!

 ## BRIGHT IDEA:

Take time out to watch funny films, clip out cartoon strips in the paper and collate them in your journal, tell jokes, laugh out loud for no reason, take regular giggle breaks at work. List five people that make you laugh and make sure you spend more time with them. Ha ha ha!

"We don't laugh because we are happy,
we are happy because we laugh."

– William James

GET OFF YOUR TUSH!

Time spent sitting is invariably time spent not moving; when you are sat for long periods of time you shut down metabolically, your circulation becomes sluggish and your brain becomes foggy. Even if you have exercised for 30-60 minutes every morning, if you spend the next six to eight hours sat on your 'tush' it's a health hazard. The so-called 'sitting disease' has been compared to smoking – and when doctors start comparing anything to smoking it's time to stand up.

Make sure you break up your sitting down times with periods of activity to reactivate your glutes. Take a walk, stretch, jog on the spot, do a few squats, get up and get moving otherwise you will end up with a big, numb tush – you know, the ones writers get from sitting for hours as they work on their manuscript, something I now relate to! When you take active breaks every 60-90 minutes you will get your work done much faster with a clearer head, more energised body and your glutes will thank you for it.

It might seem like a paradox, and the last thing you might feel like doing when your energy levels are low, however a brisk walk is one of the best natural energisers around. It boosts circulation and increases oxygen supply to each and every cell in your body, helping you to feel more alert and alive. It wakes up stiff joints and eases muscle tension so you feel less sluggish. If you find that you have energy slumps at work, drink some water and head out for a walk at lunchtime instead of sitting in a café or at your desk, sit in a park, close to nature and see what a difference it makes. You will be able to move mountains when you get back to work.

Research shows that adding 150 minutes of brisk walking to your routine each week can add 3.4 years to your lifespan; get your 10,000 steps or more in daily and track them with one of the many fitness gadgets on the market.

BRIGHT IDEA:

If you like dancing and walking, combine them and go 'dance walking'! Play the Pharrell Williams *Happy Song* and dance as you walk, get everyone up to join you; like smiling and laughing, it's contagious and will be a massive Chi boost.

THANK YOU!

There are so many magical words in the English language – thank you ranks pretty high on my list. Wherever I am in the world I like to know at least three basic words in the language of the country I am in: hello, please and thank you – when delivered with a smile they can make a big difference. We live a life full of things to be grateful for: comfortable homes, decent clothes, food and water, transportation, access to healthcare and education. A good life that brings with it a lot of freedom, safety and security; the question is, are we grateful for it or do we take it for granted? An attitude of gratitude is a life-long mindset. Besides, when you're grateful it boosts your energy, the kind you need to move and climb mountains!

BRIGHT IDEA:

From now on, every day, say *thank you, thank you, thank you*, think of all the people, places and things you are grateful for. Make sure YOU are in your thank you list and carve out time to thank those who have helped you. Start a gratitude list in your journal and jot down at least three things you are grateful for every day – yes EVERY DAY! The more times you say thank you, the more things you will have to be thankful for.

By the way, every birthday I call my parents and say thank you for the gift of life. I know some people think it's a bit weird to say 'thank you for having me' on my birthday; however I highly recommend you do, your parents will appreciate it too.

When I was pottering through the shops in Kathmandu I saw a scroll with advice on life from the Dalai Lama that fits so well with the topic of gratitude:

Precious Human Life

Every day think as you wake up.

Today I am fortunate to have woken up.

I am alive

I have a precious human life

I am not going to waste it

I am going to use all my energies to develop myself,

to expand my heart out to others,

to achieve enlightenment for the benefit of all beings

I am not going to get angry or think badly about others.

I am going to benefit others as much as I can.

What great advice.

DO YOU HAVE ENOUGH FUN?

It's really important for children and adults to **PLAY** – period!

Play for adults, unless it is competitive sports, is often dismissed as being silly and unproductive. We are conditioned that once we reach adulthood it's time to 'get serious'. Besides, there's no time to play between all your personal and professional responsibilities. If this is true for you it's time to change. The minute you stop playing you start dying. We never lose the need for joy, pleasure, novelty and creativity – ever!

Being more childlike helps you to be more creative, more imaginative, more innovative and more open to a world of possibilities. Next time you want to learn something new take a childlike approach to it and see how different it feels.

Children are naturally curious; they ask heaps of questions, live in the present, say what they are thinking and find it easy to get lost in play. As we grow up we lose this sense of childlike play. To regain this sense simply observe children, play with children, talk to them, ask them lots of questions. If you don't have kids play with children of friends, offer to take them out, go watch a fun movie, read books, play make believe, pull out the colouring books, build sandcastles, head to the bouncy castle, go to the zoo or a water park. Ask lots of why and what if questions. Fun isn't just for kids or for the weekend, it's a choice and an attitude so when life gets too routine or serious it's time to press PLAY. At the Virgin Megastore close to where we live they have a bright red pipe slide going from the first floor to ground level and I love sliding down it for fun. Going to water parks is another "playtime" for me, going with the flow of the water and letting any worries wash away with it is therapy in itself. Where do you go to play when life starts weighing you down?

Joyful play is like food and water – it's my oxygen! Give yourself permission to play every day and encourage your children to play – preferably outdoors, not on a Play Station. Most of the stress experienced today is a result of our disconnection from nature and over attachment to technology. Nature deficit disorder is so common these days so please make sure you go out and get a fix of nature every day.

YO YO'S – HOPSCOTCH – PEASHOOTERS

Pause for a minute and think about what things brought you happiness as a child, often it's the most simple pleasures of life that bring you joy. What games did you play as a child that you really loved? Can you recreate them today? I had a bright red yo-yo, a pea shooter and loved playing hopscotch. I spent lots of time playing outdoors with no sign of any technology! We lived near a farm so I loved going out to play in the fields, climbing trees, telling stories, playing tag, hide and seek, running barefoot and playing make believe. Wind back the clock and do some of the things that brought you joy as a child.

How can you be fun to be around if you are not having fun? Get outdoors as often as you can. Nature is a great energiser. When you are in different countries you can have fun just by following some of the traditions of that country – like the onsen ritual in Japan that Carol and I tried out after summiting on Mount Fuji!

> There is a certain etiquette when it comes to experiencing an onsen (Japanese hot spring bath). Virtually all onsens are 'nude only' baths. Before you step into the waters, you must wash yourself thoroughly while seated on a small stool. Your wash cloth shouldn't enter the onsen water. You also can't leave it sitting at the showers. Many people place the towel off to the side of the bath beside them. And so what brought Jules and myself joy and laughter that day was sitting in the onsen stark naked, the hot water easing any aches and pains out of our muscles, and as the Japanese would do, with a flannel on our head.
>
> Carol Talbot, author of Hitting the Wall and Breaking Through

CLEARING OUT CLUTTER GIVES YOU ENERGY

Clearing out places and spaces is a great way to move stagnant energy around, it's a fun way to burn some extra calories, find things you didn't even know you had, or thought you had lost, and most importantly allows new energy to come into your life or simply gives you more space.

When Calin and I moved from Dubai to Hong Kong we had 1650 cubic feet of household contents. Calin is a bit of a squirrel and gets separation anxiety the minute I start talking about getting rid of things. Apartments in Hong Kong are considerably smaller than in Dubai so we had a real challenge finding a place for everything and ended up taking a much bigger place than we needed as a couple, just to accommodate everything.

When we moved again in 2012 we made a pact to let go of a lot of things and got our final shipment down to 850 cubic feet. We agreed that we would go minimalist in our next home, no more purchases of fridges, cookers, washing machines or wardrobes allowed. We found a place in Abu Dhabi that has fitted wardrobes and already has all the kitchen white ware. The rule is that for new things to come in something has to go out.

Give one thing away every day for a month and see how much better and lighter you feel…

Physical clutter is easy to identify. Mental clutter can be more difficult to recognise. Thoughts are energy so if you are holding onto resentment, past hurts or find yourself running the same thoughts over and over again it can create energy blocks and eventually lead to a build-up of stress or physical problems in the body. Check out the Louise Hay book *You Can Heal Your Life* for an in depth look at how your thoughts can impact your body.

One way to release your thoughts and clear what I call a "monkey mind" is to start a journal. Putting your thoughts in writing is a simple outlet to help eliminate the clutter in your mind. Another way to release mental clutter is to let distracting thoughts out of your mind and picture them floating away on a cloud. Focus on your breathing as you do this and let your mind and body relax more with each breath.

LIGHTEN YOUR LOAD

There are four questions to ask yourself when it comes to holding on to something:

1. Do I use/need it?

2. Do I love it?

3. Does it bring me joy?

4. Does it have a high sentimental value? (hard to be objective on this one!)

If not – LET IT GO!

When I pack for expeditions I take exactly what I need, no more, no less. The higher and further you go up a mountain, the lighter your backpack the better. It's the same in business: the higher up the career ladder, the more you need to let go to your team so you don't get bogged down in the details. Let go gracefully and trust.

RE-ENERGISE AND SIMPLIFY YOUR LIFE

Getting organised and staying that way is a great way to simplify your life and conserve energy for the things that matter most. I highly recommend you do a regular 'clean sweep' on your life and the places you spend time in; you will be amazed how much more energy you will have – not to mention a clearer, lighter head (bye-bye monkey mind!). Doing this makes moving on easier too. Time to open your journal…

- Make a list of all you have to do

- Make another list of all the things you will stop doing (the time-wasting, non-purposeful stuff that takes you away from your primary focus)

- Plan your time wisely and note down all appointments and commitments in your diary/iPad/phone, make sure you have 'me time' appointments to reconnect with yourself (having back-to-back meetings with no time in between is not smart)

- Clean up your house and office, donate, sell, dump anything that does not bring you joy, that you do not use, need or love

- Clean out your car and get it serviced (do this for your body with a detox and get all your health screening done)

- Clear off your desk – only keep what you are working on

- Organise all your papers, accounts, insurance and wills

- Create soft copies of important documents

- Automatise payments for all your bills

- Keep all your business/financial books in order

- Review any projects you have started and not yet finished or have been going on a long time; decide whether to do them, delegate them or dump them

- Return anything you have borrowed – and ask for anything you have loaned out back (unless you don't need or love it anymore!)

- Let go of the old and make way for the new

No time to do this? Delegate it to someone who would love to do it for you, and pay them in cash or in kind. The only exception to this option is your mind and body – that's for you to sort out!

OK, it's time to switch off again, you know the routine.

1. **MEDITATE**

2. **COME TO YOUR SENSES**

3. **AFFIRMATION**
   I am Joyful and full of energy

4. **POWER OF THREE**

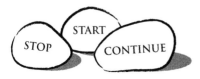

What are you going to start, stop and continue doing as a result of reading this chapter?

What's your 'WHAT BRINGS YOU JOY GIVES YOU ENERGY' STORY?

Write it now!

What are you excited, committed and grateful about in relation to this chapter? Jot your thoughts down in your journal or on the Notes pages at the end of the book – and then move on to the next chapter!

LISTEN TO
YOUR HEART

LOVE IS THE ANSWER

*"Let yourself be silently drawn by the
strange pull of what you love.*

It will not lead you astray."

– Rumi

NEVER ENDING PEACE AND LOVE

Part of this chapter was written during a mountain retreat in Nepal. If you have not been there, I highly recommend a visit, especially in the autumn or the spring when the weather is perfect for trekking. My first visit to Nepal was in April 2003 co-leading the Everest Base Camp women's trek with Jannike. One of our guides, Dhorje, asked me what I thought Nepal stood for; I came out with a list of things I associated with Nepal. His answer was simply 'Never Ending Peace and Love!' He then proceeded to let me know that Japan stands for Jumping and Pumping All Night – love it!

To move mountains, access the mountain in you and climb a mountain takes time, energy, focus, discipline and LOVE. Let's take a look at love...

Everyone defines love differently. It's a special yet complicated emotion that is relationship, environment and context specific. There are many different forms and styles of expressing love – it's not a one size fits all. The Ancient Greeks had many words to describe love so let's take a look at some of the most powerful ones that make the world go round.

Agape is the unconditional love of humanity, it's the love that accepts the recipient for whom he or she is regardless of their flaws or short comings. This form of love is all about giving and expecting nothing in return. When you see or hear of a crisis in your home town or around the globe this type of love calls you to give your time or money to a charity or relief fund. Think about the times you have been compelled to reach out and help someone out of love for the human race – this is Agape in action.

Phileo relates to a warm, platonic, affectionate love between friends, co-workers and team members with shared goals and missions. There is plenty of Phileo love on Mountain High expeditions and retreats as a result of sharing experiences and working as a team towards a common goal such as climbing a mountain.

Storge relates more to family and close friendships. It's the love parents have for their children, the love brothers and sisters have for each other or for their aunties, uncles or grand-parents. It can also be the deep caring and attachment that best friends share. **Ludus** refers to a more playful, flirtatious type of love and **Eros** is the passionate intense love that triggers "high" feelings in a new relationship. Staying madly and romantically in love can be short lived or it can develop into **Pragma**.

Pragma is love which endures. Think about couples who have fallen in love and stand together in love over a long period of time or lifetime friends that look out and care for each other. Relationships are the meeting of two whole beings, not two halves completing one another.

It's clear that there are many forms of love in relationships, business, sport and life. When you hear someone say "I love chocolate, I love music, I love that dress, I love the way you do that or I am love–sick" you can see how easily love can be confusing! Love is a gorgeous word, use it more meaningfully.

"Words sometimes get sick and we have to heal them."
– Thich Nhat Hanh – Teachings on Love

Love is complicated, simple, kind, blind, giving, a kiss, gentle, music, food, people, the opposite of fear, it keeps you young. Love is beauty, unexplainable, gives you energy, makes the world go round – it's all you need. Love is you, me, us, the birds and the bees, a teddy bear, songs, books, poems, films, roses, chocolate, jewellery, a place, a goddess, a heart, a light within, the fire in your belly, Valentine's Day… the endless list goes on!

In very simple terms love is the universal glue that holds everything and everyone together through thick and thin, it can inspire and gives us the courage to achieve the extraordinary.

HOW CAN I ACT WITH HEART

Once you have defined what love is and means to you, love will find its way to you. What is it about certain things, people or places that makes you love them? What makes you fall in and out of love? How do you measure love? These are big questions and there are so many answers to this magical, crazy little thing called LOVE! There is not one clear-cut answer to the question of love – yet love is the answer to whatever the question is! It is said that the opposite of love is fear. Whenever I have faced any challenge in business, sport or life I find focusing on love works much better than focusing on fear. When things aren't going right ask yourself: How can I put more love into this situation? How can I act 'with heart' rather than with my rational head?

Love defies logic. Take a minute now and think about what you have been inspired to do in the name of love.

M.A.D. L.O.V.E.

When I first started Mountain High I came up with the concept of love as being Lots Of Valuable Experiences; the mission was, and still is, to offer lots of LOVE (valuable experiences) to people by speaking about and offering expeditions, retreats and workshops. Add M.A.D. to the equation and you get MAD LOVE – making a difference through lots of valuable experiences. Being MAD means being someone who makes a difference to themselves, to others, to nature, the community, a cause, or simply to the country being explored by supporting tourism there. Mountain High is Love in Action and my action plan is to create more LOVE for everyone!

Shared experiences in new environments bring people even closer together, strangers become life-long friends, and couples/families get to connect at an even deeper level. Travel and exploring new places is a great opportunity to fall in love with the world again, to spend quality time with yourself, others and with nature.

BRIGHT IDEA:

Open a LOVE account and make regular deposits into it. I suggest at least 10% of whatever you earn, this is your save to spend account, spend it on something that you have always wanted to do and love doing.

WE ARE A FAMILY – CAMINO CONNECTIONS

I ran a trip to walk the last 110km of the Camino De Santiago trail in 2015. Eighteen people signed up to include a gorgeous family of four. Reem had climbed Kilimanjaro with us the previous summer and mentioned that she would love to walk the Camino with her husband Ramzi and her two sons Gabi and Karim. I was delighted when all four of them signed up. I loved to see how they supported each other along the way; when one was feeling tired or low, the others would lift them up, other times they walked apart yet always in sight of each other. Reem commented that this was one of the few times that they all were able to get to know each other on a completely different level, to really come together as a family again. Full-time jobs and studying overseas means spending lots of time apart for many families. Reem has some wise thoughts on love and family.

> *Love, family and friends are the essence of our lives, cherish them and keep them in your hearts. Life is a beautiful journey and every day is a miracle full of new beginnings and promises. If there is anything I would most like my children to learn and know, it would be to love and love wholeheartedly – love opens the way, helps us realise our dreams and makes the world go round.*

Reem Ghannoum

THE GREATEST LOVE OF ALL

Love is one of the most healing, powerful and harmonising energies in life. Being able to give and receive love without conditions or attachment impacts every aspect of our life. The simple act of smiling, giving a helping hand, a hug, some advice, a listening ear, especially in times of need, are all acts of love. The greatest love of all is the love that lies deep within ourselves for ourselves, it's our first and last love. Do you love you? The correct answer is yes. I know there are times when you might say no or maybe. Sometimes you only say yes when things are going well for you, sometimes you look to others or to things for love, the truth is love is YOU... love yourself first and FOREVER.

When times are challenging it is even more important to love yourself. Love yourself enough to care about how you live your life, what food you eat, how you look, who you spend time with, what books you read and the work you do. The big question is do you love yourself enough to be able to get back up every time you get knocked down? Anything is achievable when love is your driving force.

> *"Don't let your happiness depend on*
> *something you may lose."*
> – C. S. Lewis

It's important to love yourself enough to help yourself. It's easy to become needy and overly dependent on others or on things for your happiness; the question is what happens when they are no longer there? Besides, if you don't love yourself how do you expect others to love you?

> *"Love yourself first and everything else falls into line.*
>
> *You really have to love yourself to get*
> *anything done in this world."*
> – Lucille Ball

> *"To love oneself is the beginning of a lifelong romance."*
> – Oscar Wilde

BRIGHT IDEA:

Stop reading for a moment, grab a pen and your journal and write your 'what I love about me' list, then write a list of all the things you do to nourish your self-love. This exercise might be hard for some people, maybe you think it's selfish to love yourself first? You can only give what you've got – when you have love you've got the lot!

YOU ARE SPECIAL

See and think of yourself as a majestic mountain. Mountains have strong foundations. Make your foundation one of self-love – that is where your power lies. There is a person with whom you spend more time than any other, a person who has more influence over you, and more ability to interfere with or to support your growth than anyone else. This ever-present companion is YOU. You are the most important mountain in your life so make sure to treat yourself that way – here are a few tips to get you started:

Nourish yourself and eat foods that fuel your mind and body to be healthy and strong. Exercise and stay active to keep your body fit and strong. Physical activity lowers stress hormones and boosts the feel good hormones in your body. Choosing an activity you enjoy means you are much more likely to stick to it. Stay away from energy drainers and naysayers; instead make sure you have regular connection with people who support you to feel good about yourself. Spend time every day to be alone with yourself, if you can't be with yourself how do you expect others to be with you? Quiet your mind through meditation, take a mindful walk in nature to focus on the natural beauty of the world and simply pause to listen to your thoughts and feelings. Set healthy boundaries and get better at saying no to others so you can say yes to yourself.

My dear friend Pansy knew when to say no so she could say yes to her health when she made the decision to turn around on a summit push on Kilimanjaro. A few days into the trek she had a serious groin strain that made it very difficult to walk. Despite this she took one step at a time and made it up to well over 4,500 metres. Most people wouldn't make it up a flight of stairs with a groin strain. She made the tough love call of turning around at 2am in the morning on the summit push knowing that to go on would cause long-term damage to her body. Out of self-love, Pansy did what was right for her body at the time, this takes courage, compassion and setting healthy boundaries. In her own words, *"One's achievements and worthiness does not depend on acknowledgement from others"*.

If you tend to be your own harshest critic practice being less hard on yourself when you make a mistake and remember to celebrate and honour all your achievements however small or big they are. Loving yourself doesn't mean you have to stop improving yourself, it means accepting your perceived dark and light sides, your unique qualities and potential. By treating yourself well you show others how to treat you. Focus on your strong points instead of worrying about your imperfections or perceived weaknesses.

DAILY – DAILY –DAILY

Just by choosing one or more of these self-love actions on a **daily** basis you will improve your physical, emotional and psychological state. I stress the word **daily** as it takes time to build unshakable self-love. Do something for yourself every day, not just on your birthday or special occasions. Look after your mind, body and spirit simply because you are worth it.

"You can search throughout the entire universe for someone who is more deserving for your love and affection than you are yourself, and that person is not to be found anywhere. You yourself, as much as anybody in the entire universe, deserve your love and affection"

– Siddhartha Gautama Buddha

LOVE YOUR WORK

The saying goes 'love what you do and you will never have to work another day in your life'. One of the toughest things about doing what you love is to know what you really love to do. What you love to do can change over a period of time. I talk to lots of people who have changed careers several times before they really felt an intense sense of passion and fulfilment through their work. I thought I wanted to be a physiotherapist after I finished my "A" levels. My career advisor suggested it was a good stable career and would make a great choice for me so I applied and got accepted at university. It soon became clear I was not meant to be a physiotherapist. I studied hard, completed and passed my first year exams then broke the news to my parents that I wanted to transfer to the Department of Human Movement Studies and study to be a Sports Scientist. Because Dad had followed his heart in his own career he was more than happy for me to follow mine… despite it meaning more university fees.

The next three years of my student life were amazing and gave me a solid foundation for a very diverse career in the sports, health and wellness field. Instead of doing what I thought I should be doing, I did what I really wanted to do and it paid off. My advice is stop "shoulding" all over yourself and focus on what you love to do. If you wait to make a change until you are sure your friends, family or boss won't be angry you could be waiting a long time.

Wouter found that doing what you love is the recipe for freedom and made his own transition from corporate communications to creative entrepreneur.

When speaking to aspiring creatives, intent on escaping the corporate world and taking the plunge towards a freelance career or moving in an exciting new direction, my advice is always this: Do it because you love it. No exception.

Identify the creative outlet where your passion truly lies and find the courage to dive in deep. Follow the masters who've been doing it for years. Read all you can, learn all you can and just take that plunge. Follow your heart. Listen to your intuition. Be the dreamer and the do-er.

Once the decision has been made, you have no choice but to embark with gusto on the journey to get there. Doing great work requires great work. There are no shortcuts. With commitment, dedication and determination, the rewards are there for the taking. Work done with passion, motivation and energy looks, reads, sounds and tastes so much better. I strongly believe that work done with passion, motivation and energy ignites and inspires. It's the truly authentic stuff that gets picked up, goes viral and becomes the next hot topic.

There will be hurdles to jump and obstacles to tackle. Some will be small and some seemingly impossible but stick in there and you'll come out stronger. Just trust the journey you're on. Know that at any given time you are exactly where you are meant to be. Keep rocking the boat because those who only colour within the lines can't ever create anything new. It helps to surround yourself with positive and inspiring people, both in real life and in our digital worlds. There's so much great energy you can tap into, which fuels awesome work and doing what you love.

Imagine you had just ten years? What would you do?

Wouter Kingma, storyteller and creative

OPEN YOUR HEART

*"Your vision will become clear only
when you look into your heart.*

Who looks outside, dreams. Who looks inside, awakens."

– Carl Jung

When you open your heart you open the way to your own self-awakening and the ability to take inspired heartfelt action. When you are hurt, angry, fearful or feeling sad your heart closes – this holds you back from reaching out and connecting to others. Until you decide to forgive, accept and have a change of heart it's likely that you will feel disconnected. When you do something with all your heart everything flows, it's like turning the tap on after a long drought. Love is the internal energy of your heart so choose to let it flow.

When your heart is open you are:

- Peaceful

- Balanced

- Able to give and receive

- Healthy and happy

- Compassionate

- Able to express love to self and others

- Able to forgive others

- More tolerant and understanding

- More playful

When your heart is closed you tend to be:

- Resentful

- Antisocial

- Fearful

- Unable to let go of past hurts

- Afraid of intimacy

- Unable to accept love and support

- Possessive

- Over critical

- Cynical

PRACTISING LOVING KINDNESS – METTA

BRIGHT IDEA:

As with all things in life, to become skilled to the point where it comes naturally to you, you need to practise. There is a Buddhist meditation called *metta*, or loving kindness. The goal of practising *metta* is to open your heart and involves four steps:

1. First you send loving kindness to yourself.

2. Then you send loving kindness to a family member or friend.

3. Next you send loving kindness to an acquaintance or someone you are neutral about.

4. Finally you send loving kindness to someone you dislike or feel resentful towards.

Another favourite of mine is the ancient Hawaiian practice of reconciliation and forgiveness, the saying *Ho'oponopono* – meaning *I am sorry – please forgive me – thank you – I love you.*

HIGH ALTITUDE PROPOSAL

As you may remember from previous chapters, I climbed my first mountain when I was 40 – it was love at first summit and sight. Five years later I met Calin, my mountain man! He was the first man I dated that understood why I loved climbing mountains and actually wanted to climb them with me.

Our dates were mainly spent hiking, caving, diving and travelling mixed in between candlelit dinners and beach picnics. Any man who is willing to go down a cave full of bats and walk for hours on end with me is a keeper, so read on for the high altitude proposal!

ICE AXE – CRAMPONS – MILLETS

Calin and I spent one of my birthdays in Kathmandu. While we were there we decided to make plans to climb Island Peak (6189m mountain in the Everest region). The decision made it easy to choose a birthday present for me: an ice axe, crampons and a pair of Millet climbing boots – what every woman wants, right? I loved them! I hasten to add that he also picked out some gorgeous aquamarine gems and had them made into a necklace and earrings for me – a mountain Jules deserves jewels, right! In July 2008 we did a four-day snow and ice climbing course in New Zealand to test out all our gear and get up to speed with basic ice-climbing techniques.

October came around quickly and we were on our way to Lukla in Nepal where we met our guide Trijan. The days ahead were spent hiking for six to eight hours daily, each day gaining more altitude. Nights were spent in a tent – if you can live with your man in a tent it's a good sign! Finally we made it to the high camp and having acclimatised well were ready for a summit push. Just after midnight on 2 October we headed out, guided by Trijan – one step at a time! When we made it up to the snow line it was dawn, the sun was up and kissing the tops of the surrounding mountains, finally we could see the beauty of the landscape around us.

We took a short break for a hot tea then swapped our regular hiking boots for climbing boots complete with crampons, harness, ice axe, jumars and caribiners – roped up and ready! Trijan took the lead, I was in the middle and Calin was at the rear as we made our way across the snow field to get to the base of the 100m snow and ice wall leading up to a narrow ridge and on to the summit. Ropes had already been fixed on the wall and as we started our ascent three climbers were coming down on the other fixed ropes with big smiles on their faces: 'great view up there – go and enjoy it'. There was no one else in sight, we had the snow wall, ridge and the summit all to ourselves! Using the ice axe, jumar and crampons we made our way up the wall on to the ridge. Trijan made it to the summit first, I followed, then Calin.

Words can never really describe the feeling of euphoria when you reach the summit of a mountain – but what made this one even more memorable was Calin got down on his knees (not because he was knackered!) and produced a diamond engagement ring and popped the question! Now I realised why he had been sleeping with his backpack – it had the ring in it! I said yes – he jokes that if I had said no he would have cut the rope! Trijan was just as surprised as I was; when he realised what was happening he grabbed my camera and took a few pictures – talk about love in action! It takes endurance and courage to climb 6189m to propose; I guess Calin knew a champagne dinner would not cut it with me... that said, we did have some bubbly when we were back in Kathmandu!

Seven weeks later I was running a multi-activity adventure trip to Sri Lanka with a group and decided to add a wedding to the programme (ours!). We invited the group to stay on and celebrate a traditional Sri Lankan wedding with us at the Eden Beach Resort and Spa in Bentota, where we were later whisked off our feet on an elephant named Kumari... as you do in Sri Lanka!

APPRECIATION

"To be beautiful means to be yourself. You don't need to be accepted by others. You need to accept yourself."
— Thich Nhat Hanh

Appreciating yourself is the greatest gift of self-kindness and love. One of the founding fathers of western psychology, William James wrote that, "the deepest principle in human nature is the craving to be appreciated". Self-appreciation means not letting your flaws override all your positive qualities. Take a good look at yourself and notice how amazing you are. When you start to appreciate yourself, others, nature and life, your life improves and it won't take long before appreciation is your natural state. When I am brushing my teeth at night I look in the mirror and thank my mind and body for everything it has allowed me to do that day — walk, breathe, lift, drive, eat, swim, see, hear, smell, taste, create, speak... lots to be thankful for. Be appreciative of everything.

BRIGHT IDEA:
Stop reading, grab a pen and your journal and write a list of things you appreciate about yourself. Write another list of things you appreciate about others. Note down what people appreciate about you. Keep adding to these lists and have them where you can see them, especially when you are feeling run down and have lost sight of your magnificence.

GIVING BACK

Over the years Mountain High expeditions have offered participants the opportunity to raise funds, awareness and draw media attention to several women's health campaigns and various educational projects. It's a win-win situation when you get to travel, connect with new cultures, support local tourism and raise awareness and funds for causes close to your heart. Taking sports equipment, clothes, books and care packages to support people in need are just a few ways of making a difference. No one person can solve all the world's problems, yet you can make the world a better place by offering your time, skills, energy and resources. Giving back allows you to temporarily escape from the "rat race" and experience a different life. It can lead you on to something you might never have thought about before. One of the women who did the tandem skydive as part of the Tickled Pink series went on to train so she could jump solo and now spends many weekends jumping 12,000ft out of a perfectly good plane.

Giving back is the flip side of receiving all the love, good, blessings and new ideas in your own life. Women are really good at giving yet not always so good at receiving. Something as simple as someone giving you a compliment about what you are wearing is fobbed off with "Oh, I've had it for ages" instead of "thank you, it's one of my favourite outfits." Accept compliments gracefully, they are free gifts. If someone wants to pay the lunch bill, let them. Doing so allows them the pleasure of giving. Start to acknowledge that what you give comes flowing back to you in some form or other and that by giving and receiving you open the doors to a constant flow of energy. The fastest way to attract something is to give it.

> *"No one has ever become poor by giving."*
> – Anne Frank

Next time you see or hear about something that bothers you and find yourself thinking "someone should do something about that", that somebody is more than likely **YOU**.

You don't have to have a university degree, be Bill Gates or Mother Theresa, to make a difference. A smile, a hug, a wave, a listening ear can make a difference to someone's day. Start practising random acts of kindness and giving your TLT (Time Love and Tenderness).

GIVING AND RECEIVING FEELS GOOD

FEELING GOOD FEELS GOOD!

> *"Kindness in words creates confidence*
>
> *Kindness in thinking creates profoundness*
>
> *Kindness in giving creates love."*
> – Lao Tzu

STAY OPEN AND WILLING TO BE AND LOVE EXACTLY WHO YOU ARE – YOU ARE AHHHHMAZING!

Wherever you are right now, whatever you are facing, however high or low you may be feeling, LOVE is always the answer – so what's your question?

Time to switch off again – you know the routine, how many minutes are you meditating for now?

1. **MEDITATE**

2. **COME TO YOUR SENSES**

3. **AFFIRMATION**
   I am LOVE

4. **POWER OF THREE**

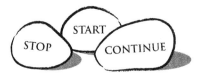

What are you going to start, stop and continue doing as a result of reading this chapter?

What's your 'LOVE IS THE ANSWER' STORY?

Write it now.

What are you excited, committed and grateful about in relation to this chapter? Jot your thoughts down in your journal or on the Notes pages at the end of the book – and then move on to the next chapter!

Moving Mountains

Discover the Mountain in You

NAMASTE

KEEP MOVING

CHAPTER 10

REACH OUT FOR A HELPING HAND

From the moment you are born you begin the journey of a lifetime, a journey no one else will travel. During your journey you will learn many lessons, sometimes hard ones. Each lesson will teach you something, look for the gift in everything you experience. Sometimes the universe keeps sending you the same lessons over and over again until you finally get the message... then you can move on to the next lesson!

"Nothing ever goes away until it has taught
us what we need to know."

– Pema Chodrun

You will never walk alone, even if it feels like it. A guide is always with you every step of the way. You are surrounded by love and beauty. When you are able to look within yourself you often realise the need to reach out to someone else for help. Throughout your journey of self-discovery you will realise that you can also offer a helping hand to others on their path and positively impact their life.

Along the way, friends, family, strangers, mentors, guides will weave in and out of your life. When you choose to follow your heart, every move you make will be a move in the right direction – and if, for any reason, it turns out not to be and you have a change of heart, know that you can course-correct. You are never lost even if you feel you are; your higher self always has your best interests at heart even when you can't quite see or make sense of it at the time!

In fact, I highly recommend getting lost as often as possible, it's a great way to keep you on your toes and 'neurally alive'. You never know what hidden treasures you will find. You and I were not born to fall asleep in one place for the rest of our lives so stay curious enough to explore and discover your place and places in the world – they might just be around the corner.

Travel has a unique way of giving you a totally new perspective on so many things; it can be a great way of finding more of yourself and be the catalyst for personal and professional transformations. Even a simple walk on the beach or around your local park can be the difference to make a difference. Spend time outdoors often, choose to be present and 'come to your senses' as you nurture yourself in nature.

Some of the best and biggest decisions I have made have been taken after a journey of some sort, be it one deep within my own heart and soul, or by physically moving to somewhere totally different and unknown. Know that every knock, fall, twist and turn you take builds a deeper layer of your character and wisdom. Cowgirl up, I know you will bounce back stronger and wiser. Living a big life means taking big decisions and chances. Sometimes you will fly, sometimes you will land on your feet and sometimes you might end up flat on your back; if so, LOOK UP, GET UP and GET MOVING... the world needs you.

"Life is like a bicycle. In order to keep your balance
you must keep moving."

– Albert Einstein

Have fun moving on, in, out, up, around and beyond your wildest dreams, out of your deepest valleys up to your highest personal and professional peaks, and if you need a helping hand to move any of your mountains, reach out and connect to our online community. There is always someone, somewhere in the world who can give you a hand to get moving with their story, wisdom and insights! No one can go back in time yet it's never too late to start NOW and create a new ending.

Life is generous to those who pursue their destiny; go set the world on fire, enjoy the journey and remember she who laughs lasts!

With love and gratitude.

Namaste

Jules xx

THE ONLY WAY IS UP

IT'S UP TO *YOU* TO GET MOVING

Book references

Chapter 3: *The Pilgrimage* – Paulo Coehlo

Chapter 4: *Dare – Take Your Life on and Win* – Gary LeBoff

Chapter 4: *Feel the Fear and Do it Anyway* – Susan Jeffers

Chapter 5: *Things To Do Now You Are Fifty* – Robert Allen

Chapter 6: *The Four Agreements* – Don Miguel Ruiz

Chapter 9: *The Alchemist* – Paulo Coehlo

Resources

Rather than overload this page with a list of websites for each of the story contributors, I warmly invite you to select the ones you would like to connect with on a deeper level, Google their names, the title of their book or their business. If you have a challenge locating them online, drop me a note and I will be delighted to connect you. Please note they will also be featured on our Facebook page and blogs linked to the book, so sooner or later you will see more of them!

Thanks to Mindy Gibbins-Klein, founder of The Book Midwife coaching programme, for coaching me through to delivery of this book.

To all the team at Panoma Press.

To Jennifer Ann Gordon, for unlocking more of my writing skills.

Namaste

ABOUT THE AUTHOR

Julie (Jules) Miles Lewis is a high-energy catalyst for personal and professional transformation. Tapping into her own stories borne from her unusual experiences across business, adventure, sports and life, she has already inspired and enabled hundreds of women and men to step out of their comfort zone and reach new personal and professional heights in the spirit of love and adventure.

Jules climbed her first mountain at the tender age of 40; at the summit she experienced a 'light bulb' moment resulting in the foundation of Mountain High in 2003. Since this time she has led multinational teams of women and men on more than 55 expeditions to 20 countries including the Arctic and Antarctica; on a personal level she has climbed 19 high-altitude mountains reaching a personal best of 7000m on a peak in Tibet.

Jules is a sought-after motivational speaker, intuitive peak performance coach and retreat leader with a passion for inspiring and enabling others to explore and unlock their highest potential through inner and outer journeys of discovery. She holds a degree in Sports Science, is a NLP Certified Coach, Certified Stress Management Instructor and is currently in practice with the Institute of Zen Leadership. Jules is the co-founder of the Women's Peak Performance Summit.

Jules writes for a number of regional and international publications; she is a regular radio and TV guest and the co-author of *The Strength and Spirit of Women* which recounts the story and images of the first team of breast cancer survivors on an expedition to Antarctica.

Jules uses a unique blend of methods to work with individuals and organisations that are consistently 'pushing the boundaries' and looking for a guide to lead and inspire the way.

She currently lives in Abu Dhabi with her husband Calin.

www.mountainhighme.com & www.juleslewis.com

Twitter @mountainhighme

#MovingMountains #TheMountain-InYou

JULES LEWIS   MOUNTAIN HIGH

Notes:

NOTES:

NOTES:

NOTES:

Notes:

CPSIA information can be obtained
at www.ICGtesting.com
Printed in the USA
BVOW11s1741260816

459854BV00004B/10/P

9 781784 520892